Baby Hunger

Biblical Encouragement
For Those Struggling
With Infertility

By

Beth Forbus

Sarah's Laughter
Christian Support for Infertility & Child Loss
A division of Shepherd Ministries

W9-CHX-551

This work is lovingly dedicated to

Lexie and Hope,
Hannah Grace,
and
Gabe, Ethan and Addie.

You are all miracles straight from the throne room of Heaven!

Thank you, Father, for giving us our laughter!

Table of Contents

Acknowledgements

First and foremost, all glory and honor, now and forever go to the All Together Lovely One, my Lord and Savior, Christ Jesus. Father, You never cease to amaze me in Your creativity and boundless love toward me! Thank You from the very depth of my being for taking my greatest sorrow and truly turning it into my greatest blessing!

To my husband, Jason. Thank you for being my stake in the ground when I turn into a yapping Chihuahua! I couldn't have survived our own struggle without you.

To Mother & Daddy. You're my loudest cheerleaders! Thanks for your support on this and every other project.

To my sisters, Paulette & Debbie. You've been my big sisters and my calm in the storm.

To Dr. Bobby W. Webster and staff at Woman's Center for Fertility & Advanced Reproductive Medicine. Your compassionate care made our journey a little less rocky.

And finally to Jana & Joyce. Thank God our memberships expired!

Foreword

Ms. Beth Forbus presented me a copy of "Baby Hunger", a manuscript written by her "with the hope that it might be helpful to some of your patients coping with the problem of infertility". I was told that it had been "therapy" for her as she struggled with the hourly/daily/weekly/monthly/yearly emotional turmoil of reproductive failure.

She told me that it was a biblically based discussion of infertility both in the Old and New Testaments. She believed it had helped her come to grips in coping with first "primary infertility" and subsequently "secondary infertility". She and her husband had moved through the Scriptures and were led to the decision to adopt a child from a foreign country rather than continue to pursue infertility therapy. They plan to raise this child along with their own biological child in the love of their Christian marriage and in His honor.

Reading the manuscript turned into a very real religious experience for me. I found myself better able to deal with couples in whom this dread diagnosis of infertility had been made. It has given me an insight to be able to discuss particular problems with a boost in my own faith and with compassion that I fear had become blunted through the years of repetition.

My life has been one of almost constant reading since I was a child. Although a "Bible student" from my childhood, I had never read the Holy Bible cover to cover until motivated to do so by the passing of my father. I did so paying attention as to how my life and those of my loved ones and patients might be affected. I clearly failed to gain the insight God gave to Beth in her search for information and peace. Beth has given me a scholarly look at the Scripture as it relates to infertility, personal loss, and the ability to put your life in God's hands with the absolute knowledge that He is always in total control. Beth bares her soul in an effort to help reach resolution and peace. First, she shares and then leads, guides, and directs those that might benefit through this quagmire of depression and desperation with a rock solid biblical foundation based on God's love and plan for each of us.

This missive shall become a cherished part of my personal library for the rest of my life.

Bobby W. Webster, M.D.
Medical Director
Woman's Center for Fertility and Advanced Reproductive Medicine
Baton Rouge, Louisiana

Infertility & Scripture

A new mother walks into the auditorium of the church with her brand new bundle of joy and is suddenly surrounded by well-wishers. At the sound of the slightest coo or whimper, squeals and giggles fill the air. Does anyone notice the young lady quietly slip out the back door and head for her car? An excited couple joyfully announces, "We're expecting!" Does anyone happen to notice the young husband slip his arm around his wife as they both drop their heads and pray that the service begins soon?

Has this happened to you? Probably way too many times. What caused your reaction? Are you not happy for new and expectant parents? Can you not share in someone else's joy? You are not selfish, uncaring people. Rather, you are the ones who face a bitter struggle every time you see an expectant mother or a new baby. You are the ones who have found yourselves struggling with infertility.

It is estimated that about one out of every six American couples of child bearing age will face difficulty getting pregnant. If you look at your own circle of friends, how many couples are fighting this fight? How many are losing this fight? Many choose to talk about it, while others keep their struggle private. No matter how they choose to cope, one thing is certain. Infertility is a most difficult battle, and we as the body of Christ need to minister to these hurting members of our family. The ungranted desire for a child can be all-consuming. New babies and pregnant women are constant reminders of what you cannot have, yet have longed for all your life. The hurt is constant. The struggle is hard. The answers are unclear. What *is* clear is that we have a Heavenly Father who loves us and understands our pain.

Sometimes, however, it gets a little difficult to believe God cares about **_me_**. If He really cared, why would He let me struggle on my own? Where was God throughout the silent years of infertility? Did He not hear the cries of Hannah as her tears drenched the dusty floor of the temple? Did He not care? What about Zacharias and Elizabeth? Surely they were "good enough". Was He waiting for a specifically worded prayer before He would answer them and give them the desires of their hearts? Abraham and Sarah were so old! How long did He expect them to wait? Did it take Him that long to figure out what to do? What about me? What about you?

The silence of infertility can be deafening. You cry out time and time again with all the strength you can muster. You beg with God, plead with God, bargain with God. Yet He chooses to remain silent. You make promises. You do all you can do. If you think He expects something of you, you do it. If giving to others would help, you would give every earthly possession you have. For some unknown reason, God seems to be doing nothing on your behalf.

If you are at the point of falling apart, may I suggest a soft landing spot? As you fall, fall into the arms of God. They are strong enough to hold you and they'll catch you every single time. For you see, when you can go no further and your strength is gone, His strength becomes perfect in your weakness. And you know that terrifying stillness in the dark times? Those times when God seems a million miles away? Even though you know He **_can_** do anything, you're just so afraid He **_won't_**. Whenever I need proof that God is working in my life, all I need to do is simply turn my hand palm up and look at the inside of my wrist.

On the insides of my wrists you can see my blood vessels as clearly as though I had no skin. Nurses love me—they never have to search long for a place to stick me! To me, these bluish tubes buried just below the surface appear stagnant. No movement. No action. To my eyes, they appear as nothing more than streaks of color on my arms. I don't feel anything. No throbbing. No pressure. They have no sound. If I didn't see them, I wouldn't know they are even there.

But what is the reality? Life-giving blood is coursing through those veins! Every moment of my life from just weeks after my conception to even this very second, blood is and has been moving, flowing, providing life-giving nourishment to every cell that joins together to create me—and it has never stopped! With every single beat of my heart, blood finds its way through the intricate highway of vessels and arteries and completes the job it was meant to do. I don't feel it. I don't have to. Just because I don't see the blood moving or feel it surging on its journey through my body, doesn't mean that it's not carrying out its job to perfection! Even if I absolutely did not believe for a second that the blood was there, my heart would still pump, my cells would still receive nourishment and my body would continue to function. I could cry, fuss and adamantly declare that I know beyond a shadow of a doubt that blood is simply not flowing through my body. It wouldn't change a thing. Not even for a second. The mere fact that I am alive is proof that blood is flowing. Life is in the blood!

Are you beginning to see where I'm headed? It's really a great destination! Romans 8:34 tells us that Christ, seated at the right hand of God, is interceding on our behalf. That Christ is seated at the right hand of God is significant, as being seated at the right hand of God designates a position of power. That means that right now, this instant, Christ, is busy working *in power* for your good. Just as you are blissfully unaware of the blood in your body flowing, working, moving through your veins, God through Christ is flowing, working and moving through the story of your life!

You may not see Him. You may not hear Him. You don't have to! That doesn't squash His ability! You may have never been aware, but He's been working on your life since long before your birth, and He's working for you even ***now***. As you read these words, He's working. As tears stream down your face, He's working. As your hopes rise and fall, He's working. As you sleep at night or as you toss and turn, He's working. As you find those few precious moments when you forget you have a problem, He's working. He never stops working on your behalf. And He never will.

Throughout Scripture we see people just like you and me who

have, on bended knee, begged God for a child. Within those holy pages we see hurting wives pleading with God for a baby. We see husbands trying their best to fill the void in their families. We see people misunderstood. We see gallons and gallons of tears. But each and every time we see God intervening and bringing hope and healing to those He loves so very deeply. There is so much we can glean from these precious, sacred words to heal the hurt and give encouragement, which the world simply cannot give. Such is the purpose of this book.

I have had to deal with infertility for most of my marriage and I'll share my testimony with you a little later. Although it was one of the most confusing times of my life, one thing became abundantly clear: the only path to peace on my journey with infertility was within my relationship with God. He showed me things I never would have seen without Him, and taught me lessons I never could have learned had I not been a student in the classroom of infertility.

Throughout the course of these writings, I want to show you couples in the Bible who found themselves immersed in infertility, just as each of us has been. It thrills me to death to realize that God looked down through time and eternity and knew that each and every one of us would need encouragement when it came to our quest to have a family. He is so interested in our lives that He included in His Holy, living, God-breathed Word infertility stories! Hidden within the pages of the Bible are people—*just like me*—who cried hot tears—*just like yours*—and fell upon the mercy of God—*just like we can*—and found help in their time of need. That's the course we take today.

Why Scripture? Why not just rely on counselors and self-help web sites? I'm not knocking counseling—that's my area of expertise! But I know that there is no problem I could ever have that the Bible isn't interested in. There are no answers that are not written within its pages. 2 Timothy 3:16-17 (NIV) says

> *"All Scripture is God-breathed and is useful for teaching, rebuking, correcting and training in righteousness, so that the man of God may be thoroughly equipped for every good work."*

God-breathed words to teach you. What better teacher about life than the very giver of life Himself! Isaiah 55:10-11 tells us

*"For as the rain and the snow come down from heaven, and do not return there without watering the earth and making it bear and sprout, and furnishing seed to the sower and bread to the eater; so will My word be which goes forth from My mouth; **It will not return to Me empty, without accomplishing what I desire, and without <u>succeeding</u> in the matter for which I sent it.**"*
(emphasis mine)

If the Bible hands you a promise, you can bank your life and your eternity on it. Need a reminder? Just go outside after a rainstorm. Has the grass been watered? Did the gush of rain you heard falling down from heaven suddenly make a u-turn about six inches above the ground and head back skyward? No? You mean to tell me it hit the ground? Weren't you shocked? I mean, come on! Water falling from the sky to water grass and weeds on this spinning globe we call home? You weren't caught off guard even a little? No? Why not? Because it happens every single solitary time it rains. Not 50% of the time. Not even 99.99999% of the time. 100% of the time it rains, the rain accomplishes the job God sent it to do. So neither can the Word of God return to Him without doing what He said it would do! It is no more foolish of us to assume that the rain and snow falling from the heavens would suddenly decide on it's own to go another direction than it would be for us to doubt that God's Word really is as powerful as He says it is and that it will do what He says it will do.

We base our encouragement to you today on the infallible Word of God. You can believe every word in God's book. God knows you intimately. You are forever on His mind and in His heart. My prayer for you is that you learn something today to assist you on this most difficult journey.

Abraham & Sarah
Holy Laughter

After these things the word of the Lord came to Abram in a vision, saying, "Do not fear, Abram, I am a shield to you; Your reward shall be very great." Abram said, "O Lord God, what will You give me, since I am childless, and the heir of my house is Eliezer of Damascus?" And Abram said, "Since You have given no offspring to me, one born in my house is my heir." Then behold, the word of the Lord came to him, saying, "This man will not be your heir; but one who will come forth from your own body, he shall be your heir." And He took him outside and said, "Now look toward the heavens, and count the stars, if you are able to count them." And He said to him, "So shall your descendants be."
Genesis 15:1-5

Abraham is known throughout history as a man of great faith and was called a friend of God. However, long before he took his place as a Hero of Faith, Abraham, then named Abram, struggled with some of the very same issues we deal with today. One such struggle was that of infertility. Thankfully, God never left Abram and his wife Sarai alone in their battle. He walked with them through the entire story.

God met with Abram in a vision and promised him great

rewards. You would expect him to be thrilled. After all, God never does anything halfway. He who created all that has ever been and ever will be created is promising a reward that even *He* calls great. And what was Abram's response? "Ho hum. Thanks. That's great. But what does it matter, Lord? I don't have a child!" Even staring great rewards in the face—can you imagine the reward that **_God_** calls great?—nothing seems to matter because there's no child to share his joy. Abram began describing the closest thing he had to an heir, but it just wasn't the same.

I want you to take some time here and see if Abram might have felt like you have, and if so, let's notice God's response. God promises Abram great things, yet somehow it's just not enough. Have you ever felt just a little guilty in your quest for a child? You look around and see how God has so abundantly blessed you with family, friends, a good church, good health, a wonderful spouse. You live in a country where Christianity is embraced and you've never had to stare down the barrel of a gun and been told to denounce Christ or die. You hear of others who suffer so greatly, have nothing or no one, yet you find yourself asking God for His personal best. Satan may try to make you feel guilty and selfish for asking God for your healing and the provision of a child when He has already blessed you with so much.

However, look at God's response to Abram when he stood at that place. Absent from this story is God's disappointment with Abram for asking for too much. Nor will you find God's anger. The omnipotent hand that flung the stars into space was never balled in holy fury as God angrily said, "I can't believe the lack of gratitude! Just see if I ever release any more blessings to you!" That's not at all what He did. Rather, He did what a loving Father does. He reassured him of His love and His provision.

God took Abram outside and in a beautiful display of kindness spoke to him in his own terms, describing for him the plan He had for his life. With the field as His classroom and the velvety night sky as His blackboard, God taught Abram a lesson he would never, ever forget. He directed Abram's attention to the stars. The very same stars he had gazed at for decades. Realize that Abram was an extremely wealthy shepherd with huge flocks. He had no doubt spent countless nights lying on his back in the fields staring up at the stars before this night. This blessed patriarch undoubtedly traced the constellations hundreds of times with the shepherd's hook that had become his constant companion. "Count them. Abram! Just see if you can! Don't forget the billions upon billions you haven't counted yet! See that star? That child will tug on your beard one day. That star? That one will break your heart. That bright star? I have a special plan there! See the one twinkling far in the distance? That child will sing my praises centuries from now! Those are your children, Abram! Your grandchildren, your great-grandchildren!" Surely there was a divine twinkle in God's eye as He watched Abram's calloused finger point skyward and his jaw drop open! The greater the number of stars, the greater Abram's lineage grew.

God used the language Abram understood the most to teach him about the things he understood the least. After God assured him that his descendants would be as numerous as the stars, don't you know he never looked at them the same again! Every time Abram got down or discouraged, all he had to do was glance up at the night sky, remember God's promise to Him and start planning family reunions!

God loves you as much as He loves Abram. You're His child too! He is not angry with you for your desire. He is not angry with you for your broken heart. Remember, He placed those emotions and desires deep within you! Rather, just as He understood Abram and the void in his life, He understands you too. He loves you. He wants to teach you and guide you throughout this and every situation you will ever face.

Sarai and Abram deeply desired a child of their own to no avail. They were human beings just like us, with desires just like ours, facing frustrations matching our own. In Old Testament times, if a couple did not have children, it was automatically assumed that the problem was the woman's. A woman who could not give her husband a son was a disgrace to the entire family. Her husband could even divorce her because she did not give him an heir. Even a daughter was not enough—it had to be a son. Imagine the incredible pressure on this grieving woman as month after month passed with no child.

Within the verses of chapter 16 I see a stark similarity between Sarai and many of us. (Before you swell with pride at the comparison, read on!) At times along my road of infertility, I could almost look down and see my feet in Sarai's dusty shoes! I thought I put on tennis shoes, but nope! There they are again. Worn, muddy sandals, borrowed from my sister from centuries ago, Sarai. It's amazing how closely my heart beats with hers! It was so difficult to deal with my own disappointment when time after time my body failed to do what it was designed to do. Like Sarai, I dreamed of a child. Like Sarai, I did all I knew to do to become a mother. Like Sarai, I wondered sometimes if God had forgotten me.

Harder still was the realization that had my husband, Jason married someone else, he would probably already have been a father. Because of me, because of the failure of my body, I was denying him the joy of a child of his own. Of course, this was nonsense to Jason—he loved me and he did not share these horrible feelings. If I ever even hinted at such, he reassured me that it was me he wanted and not another. However, Satan used this weakness in my armor to taunt me and for a while, I allowed him to do so.

Clearly, Sarai would have understood my turmoil—and yours. She watched her husband long for a child, yet remain childless. As she watched each year pass and each hair turn gray, the hurt settled in her heart a little deeper. Optimistic thoughts of "Maybe next time", turned to "It will never happen!" Be careful not to become so consumed with negative thoughts that you become self-destructive. You are fighting a difficult battle and your relationship with your spouse is one of your most powerful tools for survival. Guard your relationship and guard your heart.

Sarai had a plan to help Abram have a son—she would give him her servant, Hagar. Now, God had already made His promise to Abram that He would give him a child and surely Abram told Sarai. Somehow, I just can't see it slipping ol' Abe's mind! The image of Abram coming in from the fields several years after his encounter with God and saying "Oh yeah, Sarai. Did I ever tell you about the time…" just doesn't seem to add up in my mind! Perhaps because God didn't fulfill this promise in the flesh as quickly as she thought

He should, Sarai took it upon herself to do what she apparently decided God could not or would not do for her. When she saw the heartache her infertility caused in Abram, she did something that would seem highly irrational in our society (although a common practice in her day). She gave another woman, Hagar, to Abram to provide him a child.

I simply cannot imagine saying "So, Jason, here's my cousin for you to have a child with since I can't seem to give you one. Happy Birthday! Enjoy!" However, I know that we tend to have some very irrational thoughts and often times do some irrational things. Some of us have carried our quest for conception so much further than we were prepared to do: physically, financially and emotionally. It's very hard to be sane when everything within feels insane.

Sarai's plan to give Abram a child was successful. Hagar conceived and gave birth to Abram's son Ishmael. What did Sarai do? She was enraged! Genesis 16:4 says that her mistress was despised in her sight—even the thought of Hagar was disgusting to Sarai! She became consumed with anger towards Hagar. Perhaps she became what we would call today a "Clomi-witch"! The very thought of Hagar doing for Abram what she could not do made her incredibly furious and enraged. The Bible tells us that Sarai treated Hagar harshly, so much so that Hagar took her son and fled from her presence. Realize that this meant that the situation was so bad at home that Hagar felt it would be better to leave a life of riches and abundance and take her child and *literally* live alone under a tree!

Have you ever caught yourself feeling so jealous of those with children that you find yourself snapping at your husband or friends? Before you realize what you have done, you have said harsh, hateful words—all spilling out of a heart that is broken. Before long, family and friends find it difficult to even be around you. It's hard to remain supportive if every word you say is met with a biting response and "You just don't understand!" If you find yourself hurting this way, know that God understands your hurt and ask Him to help you be more sensitive to others (as you need them to be sensitive to you).

Abram had believed God for 24 years. Most of us have not had to struggle that long! Thirteen long years had passed from the time of Ishmael's birth. Yes, Abram had become a father to Ishmael, but Abram and Sarai still remained childless. Will a child be born to a man 100 years old? God promised a child borne to Sarai and from this child—not Ishmael—God would establish His covenant and birth many nations (see Genesis 17:19-21). But come on, God! 24 years? Even the thought of waiting yet another month can break your heart, but almost two and a half decades?

All of a sudden, one more time, God interrupted Abram and Sarai's lives. One more time, God reiterated His holy promise to Abram. God was about to do a mighty work in their lives. Don't you know that when God intervenes, everything about your life is irrevocably changed? God even changed Abram and Sarai's names.

Your struggle and your child change everything about you—even your name. As children, most girls dream of their beautiful fairy tale wedding. We get boyfriends and we secretly write and re-write our first name blended with his last. At the onset of our marriage before the first crumbs tumble from the wedding cake, some well-wisher joyfully calls out "Oh, *Mrs. Jones!*" carefully—and <u>loudly</u>—emphasizing our new name. We are thrilled to hear our new names and even giggle when we forget and write our maiden name on the forms at work. You can almost hear the buttons popping on that new husband's jacket when the maitre'd calls out "Mr. & Mrs. Smith, your table is now ready." Our new station in life involves a name change and we proudly proclaim to all we know—"I belong to Jason! That's right—I'm Mrs. Forbus now!" This new name we wear describes in a mere six letters or so my new lot in life! It's a proud moment!

At the beginning of our quest to have children, we dream of the new names we will be given—this time, both husband and wife will have the joy. We tease each other as we try on our new names like a new shirt. "Here, ***Daddy***, put this in the dishwasher!" "Okay, ***Mommy***, no problem!" We cannot wait for the moment when that precious child, with all the intelligence handed down from our very own gene pools, looks us straight in the eyes and goos "Ma-ma". Once again, the power of a name changes forever who you are.

As we become soldiers in the battle to conceive, we tend to wear our disease like a name badge. "I would love to have kids, but

I can't. I'm *infertile.*" "It's not fair that I'm *childless* and she's not!" "No children yet. We're *just a couple.*" At times we even refer to ourselves by the name of our disease. "No, I'm not pregnant, I'm *polycystic.*" Someone once said to me "Wouldn't you hate it if someone called you a 'fertile Myrtle'"? I told them that that would be one of the greatest names anyone could ever call me!

God realized the powerful impact that infertility has on a person. Flip open your Bible and thumb through the book of Genesis. Re-read Abraham's story. I'll wait while you find it! God has already promised Abram a child. However, Abram's faith would waver from time to time. After all, 25 years passed between the time of God's initial promise of a son and the final labor pain gripping that 90-year-old womb. Most of us haven't had to wait that long! But, just like us, Abram started to get frustrated. So often after the initial blow of the realization of our infertility wears off, we place our faith in God. Our resolve is so strong we will do whatever we have to— whenever we have to—in order to see our dream become reality. However, our faith tends to waver when the treatment gets too heavy, or the calendar pages have turned too many times.

Look quickly at Genesis 17: 4-6 and see what God says to Abram:

As for me, behold, My covenant is with you, and you will be the father of a multitude of nations. No longer shall your name be called Abram, but your name shall be Abraham; for I have made you the father of a multitude of nations. I will make you exceedingly fruitful; and I will make nations of you, and kings will come forth from you."

Now jump down to verses 15-16:

Then God said to Abraham, "As for Sarai your wife, you shall not call her name Sarai, but Sarah shall be her name. I will bless her and indeed I will give you a son by her. Then I will bless her, and she shall be a mother of nations; kings of peoples will come from her."

God knows the heartache of an empty nursery—yours as well as Abraham's and Sarah's. He no doubt heard the many times they cried in the darkness of the long, lonely nights, "If I were only a mother!" "If only I could hear children call me 'Daddy'!" Look what God did. It is so incredible, showing how God lives not in time but in eternity! Read verse 5 again slowly. Did you notice what I did? Read it again. He said to Abraham "...for I **_HAVE MADE you the father of a multitude of nations_**." Do you think God would get poor grades in grammar? No! God was speaking in the past tense. **_Past_** tense in response to Abraham's **_present_** problem!

God had already made him the father of many nations, yet his beloved's womb was shut tighter than Alcatraz. What did this mean? It means that God, living in eternity rather than in time as we do, had already solved the problem! He already had the answer. He already had the means. He already had the heart to solve this most pressing of problems for this couple! Long before Sarah felt the first twinge of baby hunger, God had already put His feet up on the footstool of planet earth and taken a break! He made Abraham the father of many nations long before the manifestation of that promise became flesh. Long before the first signs of morning sickness, Sarah was Sarah—the mother of many nations, and no longer Sarai, the barren wife of Abram. He changed their lives and changed their names to go along with it. Can you imagine the reaction of family and friends? You changed your name to what? Father of many nations? Have you lost your mind? Has Sarah lost 70 years off of her age? Their very names were a testimony to what God had done and was about to do in their lives.

Let's make this personal. What does this mean to you? Does it mean that God is going to make you the father or mother of kings? Maybe, maybe not. What it *does* mean is that God is not baffled by your problem. He already has the answer, and has already worked it for your good. During this time of uncertainty in your life, isn't it comforting to know that God Almighty is relaxed, in control, and working on your behalf! He has already done the work. Now trust Him for the manifestation of the answer.

As time passes with no child, God continues to repeat His promise to Abraham. In probably the most memorable of instances with Sarah, God gives His promise to her through three visitors to their home. As these holy Visitors rest beneath a tree eating the meal Abraham has prepared for them, the prophecy is given that at the appointed time, within a year, Sarah—not Hagar—will give birth to Abraham's son. Sarah, hiding in a tent, begins to laugh. Not the happy excited laugh of a woman who believes she will soon bear a child, but rather the "yeah, right" smirk of a woman who has known more disappointments in her life than she ever dreamed she'd be strong enough to bear. (It's also interesting to note that only a few scriptures prior to this incident, we see that Abraham falls on his face and laughs in disbelief when God told him he'd have a son.) I'm sure Sarah must have envisioned herself waddling through the dusty streets with a bulging belly and gray hair! The disbelief rang louder in her ears than the prophecy at this point.

However, look at the response of Sarah's holy Visitor. Just as Sarah was hiding in her tent consumed with doubt, this holy prophet—the Lord Himself—turns to Abraham and simply says "Why did Sarah laugh?" What do we glean from this? Go read the scriptures for yourself. Genesis 18:8 tells us that Abraham was sitting under a tree with his Visitors when the question was presented. Verse 9 tells us that Sarah was not sitting with them, but was in the tent. Verse 12 tells us that when she heard the prophecy given she laughed—*to herself*. I always pictured Sarah laughing out loud and the men hearing her themselves. No! That's not what happened! The Lord heard the cries of her heart even when no one else did. He hears your cry each and every time. Even when you think no one has taken notice of your hurt. He knows. He knew Sarah's disbelief at news too wonderful to believe. He knows your fear and He waits ready with the same proclamation to you that He gave to Sarah and Abraham that day.

Can you imagine Abraham here? The Lord is asking why Sarah laughed. Maybe Abraham thought his hearing was going right along with his age. Or perhaps he realized in that moment just who he was entertaining. When I get to Heaven, I really hope God will rewind the video of the years and let me watch as Abraham hears the blessed message that certainly carried him—and me—through innumerable difficulties: "Is anything too difficult for the Lord?" I envision the Visitor's eyes locking with Abraham's and with laser beam intensity speaking this confirmation not only to his ears, but to his soul as well.

Is anything too difficult for the Lord? (See Mary's story!). Is the creation of a child in a barren womb too hard for God? No! Is the adoption of a parentless child to the specifically predestined family too hard for God? No! Is a fulfilled, contented happy life without children too hard for God? No! Is peace for the childless couple too hard for God? No! Is God receiving glory through this difficult experience too difficult for God? No!

Sarah laughed and then denied it when confronted. Why? She was afraid—probably afraid that she had been caught and may have feared the consequences. We all get afraid through our infertility: afraid of the toll on our marriage, relationships with friends and family, afraid of dying a lonely old person with no children or grand-children, afraid of missing out on the joys of pregnancy or parenting. If fear haunts you, maybe you feel a little like Sarah did. Fear rises when the end of the cycle looms, so we laugh and pretend everything is okay. "Okay—so it didn't work this month. That's fine—we have a trip planned anyway. I wouldn't want to be sick over the holidays. etc." All the while the fear of holding your child only in your hearts and not in your arms grips you tighter and tighter.

Jump over to Genesis 21:1. The time had come. Sarah's barren womb was about to spring to life! The Lord took note of Sarah as He had said and the Lord did for Sarah as He had promised. (Remember the example of the rain!) He gave them Isaac ___at the appointed time.___ This is such a beautiful example of God's ultimate wisdom. He knew the absolute, exact time that Isaac needed to be conceived. Not one day early, not even one month too late. But Sarah was 90! Wasn't that too late? Not even one millisecond! God knew exactly what child would be conceived each and every cycle. He knew exactly when to allow conception to occur to achieve His perfect plan. Through Abraham and Isaac's lineage came the earthly family of our Lord and Savior Jesus Christ. Look at the people affected by Isaac. What if he had been born to Abraham and Sarah in their 20's and 30's when they probably felt he should have been? That child would not have been the same person! Everything would have been different!

Perhaps that's what God is waiting on with you and your family. Perhaps He's waiting on just the right time to bring just the right child into your womb. Perhaps He's waiting for just the right adoption to go through to bring just the exact child He has planned for you to love, nurture and raise in your heritage. Perhaps He's waiting until just the right time to give you the peace you need to know that it's okay to stop trying. Whatever His plan, as He reveals to you what you need, you can rest in the assurance that His plans are perfect, His timing is impeccable, and His heart and love for you are unfathomable.

When her beloved, promised child was finally placed in her old, wrinkled arms what do you think Sarah did? Envision this delivery room. A midwife less than half Sarah's age attends the once barren wife of this friend of God. Abraham stirs up clouds of dust as he nervously paces outside the tent. Hours of physical agony are nothing compared to the decades of emotional pains suffered by this woman. But finally after hours of labor, with sweat dripping off her elbows, the kindly midwife places prophecy in the flesh into the waiting arms of his elderly mother.

What do you think Sarah did? Do you think she cried? Did she count his finger and toes? Did she begin to count up how old she would be when he became a man, when he married? Was she so worn out that she dropped her gray head on the pillow out of shear exhaustion? Although the Bible doesn't specify exactly what Sarah did in the moments following the birth, I think I have a really good idea. In my mind's eye I see her physically spent, lying on the dirt floor and reaching for that long awaited child as his lungs fill and he screeches his inaugural squeal. The midwife looks anxiously at her patient and watches her every movement. All of a sudden, eyes wide and staring, I believe Sarah throws her head back and...cackles! Not the disbelieving smirk of a year ago! Loud, uproarious laughter! Hysterical fits of pure joy!

Can you imagine the poor midwife? She'd never had a patient lose their mind before! Should she take the child back from her? I'm sure Abraham must have burst through the tent opening to see what in the world was happening! As he rushed to her side I can only guess that she looked him in the face, handed the baby to him and laughed again! Can't you just see that astonished patriarch as his eyes dart from the red, squished and squalling face of his newborn to the cackling-mouth-wide-open face of the woman he loves? No doubt after the first few mind-numbing seconds he had to grin himself. After all, what more hilarious setting could there be than a 90-year-old woman and a 100-year-old man welcoming a brand new baby into their hearts and their home!

As she slipped from the tent, snickering to herself, I wonder what the midwife whispered to the other midwives in the camp? Perhaps something like, "Poor Sarah! All the trauma of a pregnancy in her 90's made her stark raving mad! And that Abraham! He was just as tickled as she was! They've gotta be crazy!" My active imagination shows me a scene in Heaven where God calls all the angels over and tells them to look down on this birth, saying "Watch this, you'll get a kick out of this one!" If you listen closely, I think you may even hear what I like to call "a holy snicker".

Go with me to Genesis 21:6 and I'll show you the basis for my imagination. *"Sarah said, 'God has made laughter for me; everyone who hears will laugh with me.'"* Abraham and Sarah named this child Isaac. Do you know what the name Isaac means? Take a wild guess. It means laughter! In Old Testament times, parents did not simply name their child what they did because they thought the name sounded good. They named their children based on the circumstances surrounding their conception or birth, or based on a characteristic that the parent hoped to instill in that child. Can you imagine going through life being called "God has heard me!" or "Father of many nations" like Abraham was called? "Hello 'Father of many nations', how are you today? Has anyone seen 'Father of many nations'? I've looked everywhere for him." I just love to think of Isaac walking to school one day and some of his buddies running to catch up with him and saying "Hey HAHAHA-HAHAHAHAHA! Did you get that homework done last night?" Or imagine when he met someone new. "Hi, my name is Bob. What's yours?" Isaac would have said "HAHAHAHAHAHAHAHAHEEE-HEEEHEEE, nice to meet you." Everyone that met Isaac knew that he brought laughter wherever he went.

Sarah said in verse 6 that God had made her laughter for her and that everyone who hears would laugh with her! God never does anything halfway. God masterfully turned Sarah's mourning into laughter with the birth of her son. The years of hoping, praying, and crying herself to sleep were replaced with hysterical fits of joyous laughter at the birth of this promised child and the fulfillment of this holy promise. Not only did she laugh, but everyone around her laughed too.

Haven't you ever seen someone dying laughing and before you realize it you have tears in your eyes and your sides are aching from constant laughter and you don't have the faintest clue what's so funny? God can turn your mourning into rejoicing no matter how your infertility story is resolved. And he can use you to bring laughter to someone else just like everyone who heard of Sarah's story also laughed. Perhaps you'll be there for someone else in the same boat as you. You can lend an understanding ear. Maybe you lead a support group—or will one day. Maybe you can help someone realize they are not alone in this journey.

However your infertility is resolved, God has promised all of us some things—Lo, I am with you always—with you when the pregnancy test is negative, when everyone you know has children, when well meaning people offer stupid advice. He's also there cheering with you in the good times too—when unbelievably there are two beautiful pink lines instead of just one, when the thought of throwing up actually thrills you to death! Psalm 126:5 says "Those who sow in tears shall reap with joyful shouting". Notice it does not say, "Those who sow in tears shall reap with joyful shouting, but only when their prayers are answered exactly as they planned." He promises to be with us through pleasure and pain, through infertility, pregnancies, miscarriages, adoptions, good times and bad. The Lord took note of Sarah and did for her what He promised. He'll do for you what He's promised. Period.

Jeremiah 29:11 says, "'For I know the plans I have for you,' declares the Lord, 'plans to prosper you and not to harm you, plans to give you hope and a future.'" (NIV) God placed within you baby hunger. He knows at this moment how it will resolve. He knows if you're pregnant as you sit there and you just don't realize it yet. He knows if you will conceive but it's not the appointed time yet. He knows if you will adopt and, if so, He knows which child and exactly what that child is doing *right now*. He knows if you'll never conceive. He knows the plan He has for your life and His plan is good—plans to prosper you and not to harm you, plans to give you hope and a future.

But God, how can my life and my future be good and complete until I have a baby? How in the world can it be good at all if I never have a baby? Remember what God said to Sarah when she doubted Him? Is anything too difficult for the Lord? Trust Him today—right now. Perhaps you've never had to trust Him the way you have to now. Trust Him with your heart, your body, your relationships, and your family. Trust Him with your emotions. Trust Him with your future.

Have you ever played the card game "gin rummy"? I always seemed to get paired up with the best and cockiest player on the block! I'll sit and ponder which card to lay down. With my best "bluff face" on, I frantically try to remember each and every card each player has laid down and picked up. If they look closely, they can probably even see the smoke pouring from my ears as my poor brain is trying so desperately to obey the commands I'm giving to decide just which card will win the game for me. With feigned confidence I not-so-boldly lay my card on the discard pile. Before my fingerprints have even had time to settle on the card, my opponent snatches it up and glibly proclaims "Thanks! I can use that!" I sure hope my disgust isn't showing too much! When my turn comes around again, I'm sure that I've got 'em this time! I'll hang on to what he needs and I'll throw something at him that I know is pure garbage! He'll never make anything of that! With that twinkle in his eye, he grins at me and one more time says "Oh great! Just what I've been looking for! I ***know*** I can use that!" Before long, I'm convinced—it doesn't really matter what I throw at him—he finds a way to use it!

Maybe infertility doesn't seem as easy or as enjoyable as a game of gin rummy, but there is one glaring similarity. Imagine God as the Master Player in this game we call life. Satan is His adversary. To the victor go the spoils and this time the spoils are you! One by one the cards are dealt. Satan's brow is furrowed as he studies his cards.

He's determined he'll defeat his opponent. He holds in his gnarled, vile hand disease, despair, discouragement. One by one he lays a card on the deck of your life and looks God in the face with an evil smirk. "Infertility. There God. What'cha gonna do 'bout that?" Much to his wicked, evil surprise, God doesn't even hesitate: "Thanks! I can use that!" Next round—"Misunderstanding." Once again God says "Not a problem! I'll use it to bring them closer to Me!" What? Never mind. Satan still has a few tricks up his nasty little sleeve. But one by one, the Almighty works every card into His master plan and before Satan can even comprehend what has happened, he is once again back in that oh-so-common standing as God's defeated foe! No matter what trial he throws in the discard stack, God triumphantly sings out, "I can use that!" Infertility? Not a problem. Marital difficulties? Just wait and see what the Creator of marriage can bring about! "Okay—so He can use all these things. But God, I lost my child. Even You can't use that." But use it to His glory He will. Trust Him with what you understand and with what you don't. He's never failed you. He never will.

The chorus of a beautiful song by Eddie Carswell and Babbie Mason simply says

> *God is too wise to be mistaken,*
> *God is too good to be unkind.*
> *So when you don't understand,*
> *When you can't see His plan,*
> *When you can't trace His hand, trust His heart.*

Perhaps Abraham did this better than Sarah. I thank God for a husband who was strong when I felt weak and constantly reminded me of God's promises to us. God knew you would struggle with infertility when He made baby hunger a part of your design. He makes no mistakes. It didn't suddenly occur to Him one day that you were infertile. He never said, "Oops. I missed that! Maybe I shouldn't have placed that desire in that heart." No! God has a purpose and a plan for you and for this journey you're traveling. Perhaps He wants to see if you can really trust Him with the most important aspects of your life. And perhaps He wants to turn the greatest sorrow of your life into your greatest blessing. "But God, I don't want to be this way! I don't understand what you're doing!" Listen as God ever so gently whispers in your ear—"Child, My ways are not your ways and My thoughts are not your thoughts. But I know the plans I have for you. Plans to prosper you and not to harm you. Plans to give you hope and a future."

Just like God took note of Sarah and gave Isaac to Abraham and Sarah at just the appointed time, He will take note of you and give you your laughter again.

Things to remember about Abraham & Sarah's story:

- ➤ Nothing seemed to matter without a child. Don't forget to be grateful for the blessings in your life now.
- ➤ God uses what we understand the most to teach us the things we understand the least.
- ➤ Our raw emotions during infertility can alienate us from those we love.
- ➤ God fulfilled His promise ***in due time***.
- ➤ God's provision was present throughout years of infertility.
- ➤ God can use whatever trials we face to bring Him glory.
- ➤ God can restore your laughter.

Jacob & Rachel
Choices

*Now when Rachel saw that she bore Jacob no children,
she became jealous of her sister; and she said to Jacob,
"Give me children, or else I die." Genesis 30:1*

A broken woman is on her knees, fists balled up, face distorted from too many hours of desperate longing. Her body is wracked with sobs, her heart in millions of pieces. Her husband walks in from too many hours baking in the sun-beaten fields. He sees her crying again—it's become her daily routine. At his entrance, she lunges at him, wraps her empty arms tightly around his legs. Drenched with tears looks up at the man who has sacrificed so much for her, her near panicked eyes locking with his and sobs "Give me children, or else I die!"

Century upon century has passed yet we still hear the cry of a desperate woman begging for a child. Rachel's life seemed worthless until she conceived. Not only was Rachel unable to conceive, Leah—her sister and her husband's first wife, was producing children one after the other—and they were all sons! It seemed that before Leah's baby even had time to learn to walk, he was being pushed off her lap by his mother's bulging belly, again expanding to house the new life growing inside. Time after time Leah conceived.

Time after time Rachel grieved, and jealousy took root in her heart.

Indeed, being barren in the Old Testament carried with it a much greater stigma than in today's world. A woman's worth rested in the number of sons she could birth for her husband. If she was unable to provide him with sons due to infertility—whether his or hers—or due to her giving birth only to daughters, she was often considered an embarrassment to her husband and could be put away. He was free to build a family with another woman and very often, the woman's maid was given to the husband for the sole purpose of conceiving children for him. (The wife could then claim the child and raise it as her own.) Can you imagine the pressure of infertility on these women? Not only did she have to live with baby hunger but she had the added threat of embarrassing her entire family and being abandoned by her husband. (Some cultures actually still hold to this custom, including some parts of India.)

Notice the reaction of Jacob, Rachel's husband, as chapter 30 of Genesis opens to yet another emotional breakdown by this frustrated woman. The Bible tells us that Jacob's anger was kindled against Rachel. What does this tell us? First of all, let's examine what we know about their marriage. Many marriages in Biblical days were nothing more than financial arrangements. Love had nothing to do with it. Men married women for the purpose of producing sons to help them work the field or raise livestock. However, this was not the case with Jacob and Rachel. Have you ever heard of love at first sight? How about being "totally smitten clear down to your toenails at first sight"? Read the account in Genesis 29:11 and watch as Jacob and Rachel meet for the very first time.

A servant has gone to find a wife for Jacob. After inquiring of the Lord, he returns home with Rachel in tow. Jacob had been out in the fields discussing shepherding with some men when Rachel arrived. Verse 11 tells us his reaction to laying eyes on her for the first time: "Then Jacob kissed Rachel, and lifted his voice and wept"! Can you imagine the first time you ever saw your spouse, running up to him/her, kissing him/her and then throwing your head back and bawling like a baby? That's exactly what Jacob did! That's a pretty strong introduction! He was head over heels in love from moment one.

Jacob loved Rachel and proved his love for her by working seven years of hard labor in her father's fields simply for the honor of calling himself her husband. Then after believing he had married Rachel, he removes her wedding veil only to see that in an ultimate act of betrayal, Rachel's father had given him her sister, Leah, instead! So strong was Jacob's love for Rachel that even after that, he worked seven more years for her. This was a man devoted to his wife. How many guys today would work that hard?

Given Jacob's strong love for his wife, his reaction to her desperate plea for a child may seem a bit perplexing on the surface. He was mad! He was so angry with her and lashed out at her! Perhaps he was as frustrated as she was. Perhaps he was tired of seeing her hurt. Perhaps he was just angry at the entire situation. He may have just simply been pushed to his limit and could not take it anymore.

Men are so often the forgotten grievers in the infertility story. No one to give your name to. No heritage to share. For some, the family name will stop with you if there is no child. Here as in so many other pages penned by the Holy Spirit Himself, we find a hurting husband. Jacob felt the same way many men do today. At times men are asked to carry a double burden. While their hearts are longing for a child just as their wives are, they are given the job of keeping the wife's feet at least somewhere close to the ground.

Women are typically more emotional than men and those emotions tend to spill out of every pore when baby hunger develops. Ranting, raving, tears, sleepless nights are so common for so many. But what about the men? They are expected to be the steadying force for the woman whose life is spinning out of control, but for too many, the ground is slipping away underneath them much like quicksand. "Keep a stiff upper lip. Be a man." Guys, your emotions are important. Your hurt is just as real. God knows. God cares. Don't be afraid to be vulnerable with Him. He'll never abuse this trust.

If you have ever felt the burden was just too heavy, that your shoulders are just not broad enough, you have an understanding brother in Jacob. Even though he loved this woman with his entire being, to the fullest capacity, the time came when his anger was kindled against her. Notice what he said to her. I can picture them, Rachel sobbing on her knees—again. Her heart broken—again.

Jacob has done all he could possibly do but it wasn't enough. He lashes out at her. "Am I in the place of God, who has withheld from you the fruit of the womb?"

When a man loves a woman, he tends to want to make things better for her. A better life, a better house, a better car. If a woman has a problem, she'll call her mother and talk it over but only after she has talked to her best friend from high school, her sister, and the lady at the dry cleaners. Then she takes the opinions of all of these, combines it with what the people on the internet have to say, mulls them over and just talking and hearing what everyone else had to say made her feel so much better! A man sees the same problem and decides to fix it. What does it take? How much does it cost? Okay—he's done. If fixing infertility was only that easy! Jacob had done all he could, and I believe he just hit his breaking point.

Whatever their case was, we see a marriage definitely affected by infertility. Theirs was a marriage that had survived pretty significant difficulties from the very beginning. Yet here we see a husband and wife in a "knock-down-drag-out" fight over the frustrations infertility brings to a marriage.

Perhaps your marriage has been affected by your struggle. The once joyful announcement of "We're trying to have a baby!" has turned into bitter arguments over how far to take your medical treatment, just where the money will come from, or just when to stop trying. Sexual intimacy is no longer an enjoyable act of love one for another, but it is now a scheduled, mandated necessity to achieve a desired goal. God has placed such an importance on the marriage relationship that He considers it sacred. Don't allow Satan through your infertility to destroy what God considers sacred and holy.

God has given us precious relationships with family and friends for a reason. He has placed others in our lives so that we could bear one another's burdens. God demonstrated this to me so beautifully through our hardship and struggles. Some months were particularly painful for me—the crying spells, the innumerable shots and pills, and the incredible over-abundance of pregnant women who seemed to have nothing better to do than to follow me all over town. Other months were harder for my husband. You can only stand to see the tears fall down the face of the love of your life for so long before it starts to bruise your own heart. But what a blessing it was that when I had a tough month it seemed that Jason was dealing with it okay and he would swoop in and remind me of God's promise to us that we'd have a child someday. When he bottomed out, I seemed to feel upbeat and positive and I could bear his burden for a while. When we'd both fall apart at the same time, God always sent a friend with an encouraging word or a small gift. No wonder Satan targets these precious relationships!

It seems that Rachel never quite got over her jealousy of her sister, Leah. Although Rachel had much to be happy for, nothing would satisfy her barren heart. This discontent and jealousy comes through loud and clear in the names of her children. Remember, in Biblical times, a parent did not choose a child's name simply because they thought it to be a nice name. Rather, each name had a specific meaning of either what the parents dreams were for the child, or of a special occurrence or attribute. Take some time to read through Genesis 30 and notice the differences in some of the names Leah chose for her children and some of the names Rachel chose for hers. The names tell you much about the attitudes of these women.

Leah named her children Rueben—"Because the Lord has seen my affliction"; Simeon—"Because the Lord has heard that I am unloved" (remember that Jacob loved Rachel, not Leah), Judah—"This time I will praise the Lord", Gad—"How fortunate", Asher—"Happy am I, for women will call me happy", Zebulun—"God has endowed me with a good gift", Issachar—"God has given me my wages". The names she chose primarily show a heart of gratefulness to God—"God has seen my affliction. I will praise the Lord. How fortunate I am. Happy am I. God has given me a good gift." Throughout the lives of these men, their very names made known the circumstances of their birth. Praise and gratitude for a God who knew Leah personally enough to know her own struggles and gave her precious gifts.

Now notice the names of some of Rachel's children: Naphtali—"With mighty wrestlings I have wrestled with my sister and I have indeed prevailed", Joseph—"May the Lord give me another", and Ben-oni—"Son of my sorrow", which Jacob changed to Benjamin—"son of my right hand". Now what message do Rachel's choices send? With mighty wrestlings I have wrestled with my sister and I won! You can almost hear Rachel rocking this child to sleep at night to the tune of "Nanny, nanny boo-boo!" At the birth of another son she cries "Gimme another!" Finally, as she experienced a difficult labor with her last child, Rachel died in childbirth. With the last ounce of strength she could muster, this dying woman uttered the name she would give this child. She named him Ben-oni, literally translated, "Son of my sorrow"! Thankfully, Jacob changed his name to Benjamin, meaning "Son of my right hand". How would you like to go through life being called "Ouch" or "My birth killed my mother"! "Hey, how ya doing, 'My Birth Killed My Mother'?"

Comments such as "I just think about my husband and the morning sickness starts!" are all too common. Within one weekend, you learn that your best friend, your co-worker and your sister-in-law are all pregnant. Your cousin gripes to you about how uncomfortable she is in her 37th week of pregnancy. Everyone is pregnant. Everyone but you.

It's hard to feel jealousy and negative feelings toward those you love. Relationships with people you have adored for an entire lifetime become strained. Their greatest source of joy has become a constant reminder of what you have so longed for yet cannot obtain. Does it mean you no longer love them? No. Does it mean you don't love their child? No. It means simply that you are a human being struggling with the very intense emotions waging war within your chest. Very intense emotions that your Creator divinely created and placed within you, and unbelievably, He did not do this by accident! What? He chose to include insanity as part of my being? That's what it feels like sometimes! Thankfully, He didn't leave us without hope.

Read Proverbs 16:3. "Commit to the Lord whatever you do and your plans will succeed." (NIV) If you will commit to the Lord your battle—whether it is financial, emotional, relational, etc.—He has promised that your plans will succeed. Satan would like nothing more than to see your struggle with infertility alienate you from those who love and care for you the most. When you begin to feel jealousy toward those who have children, ask the Lord to help you, commit to making a great effort on your part to overcome (remember that we are **more** than overcomers through Christ Jesus), and

He assures you in the Holy, sacred Word of God that cannot return to Him without accomplishing that which He sent it to do, your plan will succeed! That's quite an insurance policy!!!!!

Satan will try to fill your mind with negative thoughts that seem to overwhelm and control your every moment. In 2 Corinthians 10:5 we are told to take every thought and make them captive to Christ. Christ is the warden of your negative thoughts that cause you so much pain and anguish. When they are placed in His control, thrown as prisoners into a spiritual dungeon with Jesus as Warden they become powerless through the blood of a conquering Savior who loves you with a divine love so strong that you simply cannot with your mortal mind comprehend!

Imagine those negative thoughts clothed in black and white stripes, chained to a stone wall and Jesus daring them to try to escape back into your heart and mind! They are totally powerless here! There is only one sure way of escape for these damaging, hurtful words—the key you carry within your heart. You hold the key that allows them to escape the prison in which they reside under Jesus' control. Jesus is a gentleman. If you decide to take back the negative thoughts, He will often step aside and allow you to uncuff the shackles He placed on the destructive words bouncing around your heart. The choice is yours to place them in His captivity. Also is the choice yours to leave them there.

You have an opportunity through your hurt and heartbreak to draw closer to this loving Father or to turn away. God understands baby hunger better than you ever will. He is a Father who every day grieves for children who turn away, denying Him the joy of a child to love, nurture and hold close. On the other hand, He is also a rejoicing Father who loves to see a child come to Him.

Do you realize that God rejoices over you? It's true! Hurry—flip over to Isaiah 62:5—"...And as the bridegroom rejoices over the bride, so your God will rejoice over you"! Not too many bored grooms on their wedding day! Ladies, remember how your husband was towards you as you cascaded down the aisle and made the proclamation for all the world and all the old boyfriends to forever hear—"I'll take my place on his arm from now on!" Remember that sparkle in his eye? Guys, remember the butterflies in your stomach in the moments before you saw your bride? Remember the lump in your throat the size of Texas when your eyes locked and you realized that once and for all she was yours? That's how God feels about you every moment of every day. This moment. This day. With all your shortcomings, with all your hurts. That's how He feels about you and He rejoices!

Can you imagine this? You! Not the Grand Canyon. You! Not the cure for AIDS. You! As magnificent as Niagara Falls is, it's just kinda ho-hum to Him! What's a little waterfall when He has a child as precious, as interesting and wonderful as you! Don't you see the sparkle in His eye when He thinks about you! Surely you've heard someone say that if God had a refrigerator your picture would be on it!

You may drop your head at this statement and think, "Well, He may rejoice over someone else—someone who has it all together and isn't sitting in the bathroom sobbing at 2:00 in the morning because someone else got pregnant, but not me." Maybe you think He doesn't realize how weak you are. Maybe He doesn't understand how long you've traveled this stupid journey. Maybe you just kinda slipped through the cracks and He doesn't realize the tears of hurt you've shed at endless showers and baby dedications.

Do you think God is afraid of those tears? Try again. This time go to Psalm 56:8 "You have taken account of my wanderings;" He knows the path you take. He knows every struggle you've encountered in this infertility journey. "Put my tears in Your bottle. Are they not in Your book?" God knows your tears. He has them all accounted for. He knows. He cares. He's working—right now—on your behalf. And rejoicing as He works. For you see, He knows how to turn this mourning into dancing and do it so that you'll be closer to Him and bring Him glory. You probably don't know how. Aren't you glad you don't have to! Commit it to the Lord. Throw those horrible, hurting thoughts into Christ's control and rest in the knowledge that God loves you and hasn't forgotten your tears.

It seems that Rachel remained filled with jealousy and a desire for one-up-manship toward her sister. Even after God opened her womb and she experienced the joy of Motherhood for herself and not only through the children given to her through her maidservant

Bilhah, her attitude stayed the same. She still seems to have one eye on the babe in her cradle and one on her sister to see how she can do better. Even as she lay dying, negativity gripped her. No proclamations of love for her family. No instructions for life without her. No, she chose instead for her final words to be "Just name him 'Son of my sorrow'".

As you stand face to face with the issue of infertility, many choices are ripped away from you. The choice of when to have children, perhaps the choice of how many children to have, the choice of keeping your problem private. Some of the choices you do have to make are so difficult. Do we consult a doctor? How far do we go with treatment? What do we give up to pay for medical treatment? Do we adopt? However, there is a crucial area where you do have the ultimate choice. Will I choose joy or will I allow infertility to dictate my mindset and the attitude of my heart? Christ came that we may have life and have it more abundantly. We're told to rejoice, and the writer is so adamant that we rejoice that he just has to repeat himself—"Again, I say rejoice!" If you're feeling weak, the joy of the Lord is your strength. Our weaknesses showcase Christ's ability to be our perfected strength.

But the choice is yours and yours alone. Christ is very much a gentleman and He will not force Himself on you. Peace that is so strong that it doesn't make sense considering your trial is yours for the taking. Abundant life is provided for you. Or a life of despondency, jealousy and discouragement awaits. The choice is yours. Do I mean that you should never cry or feel down? Absolutely not. Our Savior was a man full of emotions and the Bible even says He was acquainted with grief and bore our sorrows. What I am saying is let Christ carry those sorrows and choose the joy that runs deeper than simple situational happiness.

Remember, He has a plan of hope for your future. Whether or not that future includes children, God still holds you in the palm of His hand. He has not forgotten you. He has even written your name in the palm of His hand and He holds you there (Isaiah 49:16). Your name is constantly before Him. Abba Father is passionate about you. The choice to live a life of joy—even in the midst of infertility—is yours.

Things to remember about Jacob & Rachel's story:

➤ Jacob & Rachel's marriage was affected by their infertility just as ours can be.
➤ We can become extremely jealous of others with children, just as Rachel did.
➤ Men are often the forgotten grievers in the infertility saga.
➤ Be careful not to be consumed by negative thoughts.
➤ God delights over you.
➤ You still have choices.

Elkanah & Hannah
Purpose-Full Infertility
1 Samuel 1:1-2:26

God is a wonderful God and has given us a wonderful gift in the pages of the Holy Bible. Within the many chapters and verses are the answers to all of life's problems written with love by an all-knowing, all-powerful Father. I am so thankful that He didn't leave out the problem of infertility. Intricately woven within the stories of hope and longing you'll find men and women just like us begging God for that elusive gift of a child. Long before any one of us was ever conceived in our mother's wombs, God knew we would suffer with our own baby hunger. He knew we would crave the support of an understanding heart, so He allowed the stories of our brothers and sisters of centuries ago to meld with our own. If you find yourself feeling alone in your struggle, I invite you to search the Holy Scriptures; and I can assure you, you'll find yourself written on the pages.

Perhaps the most well known story of infertility in the Bible is the story of Hannah. We all know of her weeping in the temple because of her barrenness, and then later we find that she gave birth to Samuel. End of story. Right? Not by a long shot! Let's delve into this story and see how she and her husband sound just like us.

Hannah was married to a man by the name of Elkanah. He was

the husband to two women—Hannah and Peninnah—as was customary in their day. Now, can you possibly begin to imagine what it would be like for your husband to have two wives? Most of us are not even fond of our husband's ex-girlfriends. Ex-wives are usually not the best topic at the dinner table. But imagine having to share your husband with another woman in every aspect of your home life! Your house, your table, your bed. Even if there is an ex-spouse in your lives, none of us has to share our spouse the way that Hannah did. Even our laws today forbid marriage to more than one person at a time because they know that other crimes—like assault and murder—would probably skyrocket! You may be wondering where the similarities between this couple and ourselves are. Just hang in there—they will become crystal clear in a few moments.

As you read the opening verses of 1 Samuel 1 you begin to see immediate contrasts between the two women. The first is in verse 2: "Peninnah had children, but Hannah had no children." What could possibly separate these women more? One is fertile, one is barren. One is mama, one is "just a wife". One is covered with spit up and has some unknown gunk in her hair, the other is perfectly coifed. One is tolerated, one is treasured.

Have you ever felt like you were not a part of "the club"? If you have ever been to any kind of shower or ladies meeting, can you think of one single time that some woman in attendance did not start talking about her labor pains or her cravings for vanilla milkshakes? At the very least, baby pictures come out and we hear all about how little J.P. put the kitty in the toilet again. At any ballgame anywhere fathers are bragging how their child will surely make the majors and it's all because of the countless hours they spent tossing the ball to them in the backyard. As childless men and women, we tend to stand on the sidelines of the game of parenting wishing we were invited to play. I remember trying to disguise my discomfort and make a joke out of not belonging to this group by answering the dreaded question "Do you have children?" with a feigned chuckle and "No, but I have a cat!"

Perhaps you have felt alone, like you don't belong, like you're just not quite as much man or woman as they are. Look in the pages of the book—1 Samuel 1:2. Take out Hannah's name and add your own. The culture is different. The calendar is different, but the hurt and the alienation are the same.

Perhaps one of the greatest pet peeves of so many infertile women is to hear those "fertile myrtles" gripe about how long it took them to get pregnant. I mean, come on—four months is a long time! Many of us have tried month after month after painstaking year after year. There you are again—sitting right there in the temple beside Hannah.

The Bible shows how year after year Elkanah would worship and sacrifice at Shiloh. He would bring meat home and share it with his family. Although he gave portions to Peninnah and her children, he made sure that Hannah received a double portion of food because the Lord closed her womb. In Biblical days giving a double portion showed extreme love and devotion. Elkanah was making a public proclamation—even in Peninnah's presence—that Hannah was special to him and that he loved her more.

Can you visualize this scene? The table is set, the children are quieted. Peninnah sits uncomfortably for her children are crowding her. Hannah sits on the other side of the table alone. Elkanah comes in and places food on each plate. A portion for this son. A portion for this daughter. A portion for Peninnah. A portion for himself. When he walks to Hannah's place at the table he reaches deep into his vessel and scoops out a huge piece of meat. Peninnah glances over and grimaces—she recognizes the choicest piece of meat, and knows it was not by accident that it was not saved for her. Before the first bite is taken, Elkanah continues to dip. A double portion for Hannah. Was she skinny? Probably not. Was she starving? Not for love. He simply loved her more and tried to fill the void left by an empty womb.

As you walk through the valley of infertility, look around you. God walks with you. There are times He is so close to you you can almost hear His footsteps. I believe that He gives a double portion of love to you in a variety of ways. In the encouragement of a friend, in the support of a wonderful spouse or family, in the revelation He makes of Himself in scripture at just the right time. Some spouses try so hard to fill the void of infertility. If your spouse is trying like Elkanah, don't neglect him/her or his/her efforts. They may not make up for the loss, but appreciate the efforts. God knows what you need and when you need it. He will provide your double portion when the circumstances of your life dictate.

The Bible specifically tells us that Hannah was infertile because the Lord closed her womb. It may seem troubling to read that *the Lord* closed Hannah's womb. This tells us that He not only *allowed* her infertility, but *caused* it! He purposefully allowed Hannah to become infertile. In fact, it bluntly says, "the Lord had closed her womb." What does that mean? Did it mean she had committed some horrible sin and this was her punishment? No. There's no mention of sin anywhere in her story! God *purposefully* closed her womb. Purposeful infertility! Break the word apart. Hannah's infertility was purpose-full! God had a mighty purpose and plan for this struggle. That makes it holy! Your infertility, as hard as it is, can bring glory to God! God could have reversed it. He could have forbidden any infertility and Hannah's womb would have been incredibly fruitful. He could have forced Peninnah to stop her torment. He did not. This tells you that God wanted to use what hurt Hannah the most to bring her closer to Him. It may be impossible at this time in your life to see how God could use the most distressing situation you have ever personally encountered, but God is an incredibly creative God and He has promised to turn your mourning into dancing. Trust him and hang in there.

You can see how Elkanah's favoritism would cause problems for the women sharing the house and sharing the man. Surely they were not the only women to get a little snippy when things didn't go right. The Bible tells us Peninnah bitterly provoked Hannah in order to irritate her. She knew that Elkanah loved Hannah more. His double portions and extra attention made it obvious. Jealousy was as much a resident in this home as the women were! Peninnah couldn't have Elkanah, but she had what Hannah wanted more than anything in the world—an active healthy womb—and flaunt it she did! Perhaps Peninnah sang lullabies when Hannah could hear— even if the baby wasn't sleeping. Did she leave toys around where she knew Hannah would relax in the morning sun? No doubt when Hannah entered the room, Peninnah would "absent-mindedly" rub her ever-expanding belly and loudly gripe about the weight or discomfort. And let's not forget how she probably described in excruciating detail every little kick or hiccup. In fact, her provocation was probably more direct—more "on purpose" than accidental. "That's right Hannah! I was sick again this morning! Maybe it will be twin sons this time!" "What's the matter Hannah? Crying again? Is your double portion upsetting your stomach?"

Even though most of the hurtful things flung at us are not intentional, the sting is no less painful. You have certainly walked into the office in time to hear a co-worker griping about swollen ankles when you know you would be proudly showing them off to anyone who would look. Well-meaning parents and in-laws will jokingly—sometimes not so jokingly—ask or pressure you—"When am I going to have grandchildren?" If you've ever felt that no one understands you, simply leaf through the pages of this Holy book. Hannah's infertility and Peninnah's attacks lasted for years. It happened *__year__* after *__year__*. If you've struggled with infertility for so long, you have an understanding sister nestled within the pages of 1 Samuel.

1 Samuel 1:8 shows us the portrait of the hurting, frustrated husband. Once again, Elkanah finds Hannah weeping. Once again, he just can't make the hurt go away. His frustrations finally explode! "Am I not better to you than ten sons?" He tried to make Hannah happy. He cared but felt left out and hurt. Perhaps he didn't quite understand the depths of her grief or the void. He was a father; she was not yet a parent. Women are often the focus of infertility treatment and support. Most of the time, the physical problem is the woman's; so as the medical focus is on her body, the emotional focus is on her heart. Isn't it wonderful that the Bible recognized infertility as a man's problem as well as a woman's! (See Deuteronomy 7:14) Don't forget that your husband hurts, too. Elkanah is suffering the same hurt as his wife—and he even has other children!

Verse 10 shows us the Hannah that so many of us are familiar with and can so easily identify with. The Bible says she was ***greatly distressed***, and in ***bitterness of soul*** makes her way to the Lord's temple. Her hurt has not gone away. Her womb is still barren. However, Hannah made a crucial decision that led her to the turning point in her story. She made the decision to face her problem head-on with prayer. No matter how severe your problem is or how many choices have been taken away from you, you can always choose to pray. What power in this universe is more powerful? Prayer can open blocked tubes, reverse diseases, lead us to the right people, lead us away from others and calm hurts and indescribable fears. If you have not saturated your infertility story with prayer I so strongly encourage you to do so.

Still greatly distressed, Hannah prayed to the Lord as she wept bitterly. How many nights have you wept bitterly because your womb and your nursery are still silent? You're a modern day Hannah! The Bible doesn't say she cried. She passed that years ago. Here we see a woman shattered by her grief, so overcome with sorrow that she can no longer stand—not figuratively or literally. Her cries to the Almighty started out strong but from sheer repetition, they've dwindled to nothing more than a raspy whisper. Tears are gone, for there are no more to shed. She feels as if the soul inside of her would die if one more cycle passes without new life.

Verse 12 begins this way: "As she kept on praying..." Notice that this does not say the answer to her prayer was made manifest the first time she prayed. Or the second. Even through countless months and years of infertility, even through a myriad of unprovoked attacks from someone in her own home, even with her prayer seemingly yet unanswered, Hannah kept on praying. If you have seen yourself in Hannah's story thus far, I pray that you will see yourself in her faith in an unseen God. The infertility lasted. So did Hannah. The provocations kept coming. So did Hannah. In the midst of her heartbreak, Hannah kept on. I know her faith moved the heart of God. Eventually the answer to her prayer was delivered into her womb and a child was born. I pray that in the midst of your heartbreak you'll keep on calling out to God. Ask Him for wisdom, guidance, and peace. You'll find He'll answer your prayers.

People often make reference to unanswered prayer, but in actuality there is no such thing. Sometimes God, in His wisdom says "No". Sometimes He says, "Wait". Although they are not the answers you're hoping for, they are both answers. I'm not sure which is harder, but I know God hears and answers every single prayer. He is aware of every tear you have shed. From the very first one that slipped down your cheek when you first began to suspicion that something was just not quite right to the ones you cried this morning. And remember, He even keeps them bottled up for you.

In the temple where Hannah prayed, there was a priest named Eli. As Hannah wept in the temple the priest stood on the sidelines watching her. By this time, Hannah had been making her petitions known to God for so long and with so much passion that she had no voice left to be heard. Not even a whisper. Her cries were silent to man, but as thunderous as a mighty river to Heaven. Eli watched her for a while and began to create his own opinion about her. "She must be drunk! Why else would she stagger into the temple and fall in the floor? Why else would her tears reduce her to nothing more than a pitiful mound of humanity?" Misunderstanding. He went so far as to scold her and tell her to put her wine away.

Can you imagine the hurt? Someone who should have been compassionate, or at least not caring one way or the other, makes a horrible blunder and hurts you further. Not quite so unbelievable when you think of it. "Stop drinking Hannah!" Much like "Stop stressing and relax—it'll happen". "I'm sorry you miscarried, but at least...!" Sound familiar? For those who have never experienced infertility, misunderstandings are common. Not intentional, but too frequent. But like Hannah, when we are misunderstood we are forced to the place where we must defend the intensity of our desire to have children.

Hannah explained to Eli that she was not drunk but oppressed in spirit, deeply troubled and had poured out her soul before the Lord. She asked him not to consider her worthless. She must've had reason to feel this way. Perhaps the way he approached her or spoke to her. Maybe their culture. Although the times are different our hearts are not. "We're just a couple, not a family". Again, as I've mentioned before, I think it is as important to notice what is missing from Scripture as it is to see what is there. Look where we see God's anger. Did you miss it? Look again. That's right. It's not there. What about God's disappointment in Hannah for her tears, her despondency? It was Eli who looked down on her as a drunk. God did not. You are no less worthy, no less precious or dear to God because you are barren. You are His child and you have infinite worth in God's economy. We often feel that nothing will be right until we have a child because we are simply not complete. God says differently. We are complete in Him. Our worth was made perfect in Christ's sacrifice on Calvary.

After this encounter with Eli at the temple, you see some differences in Hannah. In verse 18 we are told that she ate something. If you glance back at verses 7 and 8 we are told that she was so downcast she could not eat. We are also shown in verse 18 that her face was no longer downcast. Can you see this in your mind's eye? Imagine Elkanah's surprise! Here was the woman he cherished. He had watched her suffer year after year. He certainly must've expected the same of her this day. Visualize this: Elkanah sits down with Hannah to eat. He scoops out her double portion half expecting most of it to go to the dogs. All of a sudden he hears some strange smacking. Who is that? Are the dogs already here to get their dinner? He looks up and in the most surprising turn of the day, realizes that it is Hannah hungrily wolfing down her food! She hasn't eaten like this in years! She notices him looking at her and amused at his expression, smiles sweetly—a smile he has missed for so long—and takes another bite!

What made the difference? I believe Hannah had a true encounter with God that day. She worshipped God in the midst of her hurt, much like David when he lost his child. I believe she once and for all turned her heartache and her infertility over to God that day. When you've carried a heavy burden for so long, can you imagine how free you feel when it is finally lifted? He's so much stronger than you are—let him lift your load for you. Perhaps like Hannah, you'll get your appetite back—your appetite for life, for fun, for freedom of worship, for relationships soured by your endeavor. What a welcome change for you as you release what you cannot carry alone!

In verse 20, we see that Hannah finally conceived a child. Much like the story of Abraham and Sarah and Zacharias and Elizabeth, we see that God opened her womb and she conceived ***in due time***. God's timing is impeccable, He knows just how and who to give a child to, and He proves this time and time again throughout Scripture. Samuel was born to Hannah and Elkanah. If Hannah grieved as strongly as she did, can you just guess how strongly she must have rejoiced at his birth! That's okay—I believe we card carrying members of the infertility club are entitled to massive rejoicing when we finally become parents!

After Hannah gave birth to her son, she fulfilled a promise she made to God. She promised that she would give her child to God all the days of his life. Now, that did not mean she would take him to Sunday School every week and read him Bible stories at night. This literally meant she would give him to God. When he was 3 years old, she took him to the temple and left him there. Not for a couple of hours or days. Not for weeks, but for the rest of his life! We are prone to promise God everything in order to try to convince Him to bless our womb. Be careful not to make a frivolous promise to God. He is faithful in His promises. You must be too.

Finally, there is one more picture of Hannah that I want to show you. After she took Samuel to the temple she made it a point of testifying to those involved in her infertility. In my mind's eye I can see her proudly standing face to face with the aged Eli explaining in perfect detail "I am the woman who stood here praying and here is the child I prayed for." Can you hear Eli ask his name? "His name is Samuel." What's the significance there? The name Samuel sounds like the Hebrew word for *heard of God*. Hannah was proclaiming that God heard her cries for a child and gave this child to her. Everywhere he went for the rest of his life, this message was trumpeted loud and clear anytime someone said his name.

Hannah didn't stop there. That wasn't enough. This wasn't some tiny, insignificant request she had casually asked God for. No—she begged and pleaded until she literally lost her voice. Therefore, it is no surprise that Hannah went to great lengths to thank God and give Him praise for what He had done in her life. Notice Hannah's prayer in chapter one where she is pleading with God for a child. It is covered in two verses. Now turn to chapter two and read her prayer of praise. It takes 10 verses! What does that tell you? That Hannah's heart rejoiced more than her heart hurt! Isn't God a wonderful God? He takes our mourning and turns it into hysterical fits of dancing!

As you read and re-read the story of Hannah and her family,

make sure that your story mimics hers not only in her faith, but also in her praise of the God who heard her cry and came to her rescue. Worship God in the midst of your struggle and don't be afraid to share His workings through your infertility story.

Things to remember about Elkanah & Hannah's story:

> God sustained Hannah throughout years of infertility.
> God purposefully closed Hannah's womb—notice—<u>purpose</u>full.
> A husband grieves for his wife.
> God grants us a double portion when we need it.
> Spouses often try to fill the void but cannot.
> Others have what Hannah craves.
> Misunderstanding is common in the infertility struggle.
> Hannah prayed and seemed to decide she would trust and survive.
> Hannah fulfilled her promise and praised God profusely.
> Absent in this story is sin in Hannah's life, the removal of suffering, God's anger, disappointment or abandonment.

Zacharias & Elizabeth
In Due Time
Luke 1:5-80

Luke tells us that Elizabeth and Zacharias were both righteous in the sight of God, walking blamelessly in all the commandments and requirements of the Lord. It was not enough to say that they were good people. Luke said they were righteous. Not only were they righteous, but they walked blamelessly in **_all_** the commandments and requirements of the Lord. Not "they tried their best", not "they did a great job", and not "they did just about everything right". Wow! Can you live up to Elizabeth and Zacharias? Well, not if you gossip. Not if you lie. Not if you overlook any command or requirement. Not if you blow it even once. I might walk blamelessly for a few hours—okay—maybe a few minutes, but before I know it, somebody cuts me off in traffic and there I go not preferring my brother to myself. No, I'm wishing he'd get a ticket for what he just did to me. Somehow I can't seem to live up to the example set by this godly couple. So why were they barren?

Elizabeth and Zacharias were not only good, upstanding citizens, blameless even in God's sight, but they worked themselves silly as servants of the Most High. Why no children? The Bible plainly says in Psalm 127 that children are a gift and a reward from the Lord. Why was this blessing and reward being withheld from two blameless people?

Have you ever felt like Elizabeth and Zacharias? Have you ever wondered why someone who never even gives God the time of day seems to conceive on accident and then acts as if their children are a nuisance to them? You've done everything you know to do to please God yet you remain childless. You go to church, pay tithes, volunteer at the local shelter, read your Bible and pray—boy, do you pray. Still no nursery, no bottles cluttering your kitchen, no car seat or baby toys strewn all over your car, no spit up stained jammies in your laundry. Perhaps you have wondered much like Elizabeth must have—Why God? Why are your blessings withheld from me and granted so freely to those who seem to thumb their nose at You?

Listen again as God leans close and whispers to your heart that His ways are not our ways. Does He love us less? Absolutely not! But God, I know I'd be a better mother! She doesn't even take care of that child! Lord, I promise I'll never treat a child that way if you'll just give me a chance. *I* love you! *I* serve you! *I* would never abuse my child the way so many do! *I* would raise my child to fear You—not curse Your Name. Why do you bless that crack-addicted prostitute and grant her a precious reward? You've made that man a father when he won't even acknowledge his child, yet my good, Christian husband has no child to bounce on his knee. Why can't we have a child?

If tears are stinging your eyes and blurring your vision as you read, maybe it's because this hits too close to home. You may have felt that God is punishing you for some wrong you have committed or perhaps punishing your spouse. You have searched your heart and still can't figure out what you have done to so anger God that He has closed your womb so tightly that no doctor, no medicine, no miracle can open it.

Allow me to make the suggestion to you that God has not placed infertility in your life as punishment. Infertility isn't the result of a vindictive God who is mad at you because you messed up. Doubtful? Look at Elizabeth and Zacharias. Elizabeth's infertility certainly wasn't a punishment. She was blameless. Zacharias wasn't childless because God was mad at him. God called him righteous.

God had a purpose and a plan for this couple and for their child.

He had an appointed time for this child to be born. This child was a child of purpose. He would be the forerunner of the Messiah! What an awesome responsibility for these parents! Can you imagine knowing you had to train a child up in such a way that his life would be recorded in the Word of God as John's life was!

Elizabeth and Zacharias were old. What if they had gotten pregnant in their youth? It would have been a different person. Not John the Baptist. Yet John was appointed ***before his birth*** to be the forerunner of the Messiah. When making the announcement of John's birth to Zacharias, Gabriel said that his words would be fulfilled ***in their proper time***. Flip the pages of your Bible open to Jeremiah 1:5 "***Before*** I formed you in the womb ***I knew you***, and ***before*** you were born I consecrated you;…" (emphasis mine) God knew all of us long before our conception. Before the conception of your child, He knows that child. He knew us, he had plans for us. If He has holy appointments laid out for our lives long before the first cells ever begin to divide, don't you think He knows exactly when our lives on earth should begin?

What if we had the authority to grant pregnancy whenever we wanted it? We might miss out on the plan of God appointed to each person before they are even born. There could be no greater tragedy. Let this sink into your heart and soul. God has ***perfect*** timing. He knows the past. He knows the present. He knows the future. He knows what's best.

Sometimes we may feel we are not good enough or perfect enough to convince God that we are worthy of becoming parents. We could never be perfect enough to "buy" a child from God. God is the **giver** of life—not the **seller**—and He chooses whom He will bless with a child. If being good enough were what it took to have children, Elizabeth and Zacharias would have had a house full of kids. We cannot compare ourselves to those who are able to so easily conceive. Why? Satan will use this as an attack on our minds to convince us that somehow God doesn't love us as much or that God has become negligent. God has infinite knowledge and wisdom and He knows exactly what our lives should entail. God is a good God. And not only is God a good God, God ***is*** good. There is no evil in God. God ***is*** all that is good. He is the source of all that is good. Everything that is good comes from Him. There is no evil, no cruelty, and no negligence in Him. Rather than being hateful and hurtful to you and throwing infertility in your path just because He's mad at you, God weeps with you when your heart is torn into.

Read Hebrews 4:15-16. We have a great high priest who sympathizes with our weaknesses and tells us to approach Him with confidence when we are in need so that we may find mercy and grace to help us in time of need. Does this sound like a vindictive Father who gets mad and tries to hurt you? Does it sound like a juvenile, spiteful controller who jerks away his toys when you don't play right? Or does it sound like a Father who wraps His strong arms around His hurting child, His tears mingling with your own, and tells you to come boldly to Him to find help in the time of your need? Not "call and make an appointment and I'll try to squeeze you in". No—He said come boldly! Run in. Burst through the doors! I'll stop what I'm doing and move Heaven and earth if need be to help my hurting child. This is the God who walks the infertility journey with you.

Look closely at the story of this couple. An angel approaches Zacharias and tells him to get ready—a baby is on the way. Watch his reaction. You can almost hear this old man gasp for air as he reaches for something to steady himself. His knees almost give way, his head is swimming and he's wondering if the glowing majestic creature is really standing in front of him or standing somewhere in his vivid imagination. Zacharias manages to breathlessly ask, "How will I know this?" Okay—a huge glowing creature suddenly appearing in my den would probably have convinced me but perhaps Zacharias had so accepted a childless life that even this was not enough. (Maybe like the infertile woman who takes 19 pregnancy tests before she finally believes she really is pregnant!) The angel Gabriel told him that due to his unbelief, he would be stricken mute until the prophecy was fulfilled.

Can you picture all the people standing outside the temple when Zacharias came out? Here he comes stumbling, trembling, wide eyed, and pale as a sheet. The crowd hushes. They know something is up—they've never seen this kindly priest like this before. The anxious crowd has been waiting a long time for this priest to appear to them and now leans in with eager anticipation to hear what miraculous message he has to share with them. The electricity in the air is phenomenal! He opens his mouth to speak, and...nothing. He tries again. Not a peep! He's making wild gestures but what is he trying to say? Something big! People are glancing at each other, their expressions as confused as Zacharias'. Before long, he shakes that graying head and walks away. For the next several months this would be the norm for him. Though he was speechless, no doubt there were countless conversations abounding in his heart and mind over the next exciting months.

God knows what you need and when you need it. I guess Zacharias needed something this drastic to convince him that God was really working and moving! If you could only see into the spiritual realm you could see how God is constantly working on your behalf. Perhaps He's gently nudging you to take the next step, or leading you to a certain physician. Chances are, that supportive friend was not placed there on accident. Your pastor's prayer that really spoke to your heart may have just been God-breathed on your behalf. Though it may be difficult to see sometimes, God really is an active participant in your life.

When Elizabeth finally gave birth to John, the Bible tells us there was great rejoicing. When people saw God's mercy to Elizabeth and Zacharias, they rejoiced with them. If God blesses you with a child-REJOICE! Let your child(ren) show God's mercy to you. Never miss an opportunity to brag on God should He grant you this gift. And never, ever forget to thank God for your child even more than you've asked Him for this child.

Notice that the very first thing Zacharias did when he was finally able to speak again was praise God! Immediately! No "Hey baby, I'm your Daddy!" No "Hey everybody—come see my boy!" Not even "Are you okay, Liz?" No. The first thing he did was to lift that scratchy voice to heaven and with joyful utterances, praise His maker! There is much to be learned from this holy man. Learn to praise God in the good and the bad times. The easy and the difficult. God made no mistakes when He wrote His Word. He let us know Zacharias' reaction for a purpose—glean from these nuggets of truth.

I truly believe that a child born from a barren womb is a special child and those who are barren are filled with so much joy at that child's birth that it is a special gift of God. Not that a child easily conceived is any less precious or valuable in God's eyes. But when someone struggles so much and is finally handed the trophy of a child, the joy and gratitude is unfathomable.

If you search Scripture for accounts of children born to barren wombs you will see amazing stories. Sarah gave birth to **Isaac**. He was prophecy in the flesh and ushered in God's promises to Abraham. **Jacob** was the product of a barren womb. The Abrahamic covenant was perpetuated through him. He wrestled with God and would not let go until God blessed him and changed his life. **Joseph** was one of the greatest rulers Egypt had ever seen and is one of very few characters in the Bible in which you will find no moral failure. **Samuel** was a judge and called as a prophet. He led Israel to victory over the Philistines, and anointed David as King. **Samson** was raised under a Nazarite vow. He was set apart for God from his birth and began the deliverance of Israel from the hands of the Philistines. These are only a few examples of the mighty works God does with the child of the barren womb. Do you realize how many children of barren wombs join together to form the lineage of Christ? Do you think God is intimidated by infertility? Certainly not! He used it to bring about the Savior of the world! What could He do through your infertility story?

Things to remember about Zacharias & Elizabeth's story:

➤ Zacharias and Elizabeth were righteous and blameless. This means that their infertility was not a result of sin.
➤ God's promise to them was fulfilled ***in due time***.
➤ There was great rejoicing when God fulfilled His promise.
➤ God can use the child of a barren womb in a mighty way

Jason & Beth
Infertility
My Sorrow, My Blessing

"I wish I was 25 so I could be married and have a baby!" How many times I had made that statement was beyond me! My sister owned a day care and I helped her in the months between high school graduation and the beginning of college in the fall. It was the perfect job for me. Babies everywhere! All I had ever wanted my entire life was to have a family of my own and that always included a husband and four children. I dreamed in exquisite detail of each child and just how perfect my life would be when I became a mother. I worked myself to death driving 1000 miles a week working my way through graduate school because a master's degree was so incredibly important to me. Yet, every time someone would compliment my tenacity and willingness to go after what I wanted I would always smile and respond "I'd give it up in a heartbeat for a husband and a child!"

I was almost 28 years old before I married. I was most anxious to "start a family." I remember the day I excitedly told my mother that we had decided to try to have a baby—"If I get pregnant the first month we try we could actually have a baby this Christmas!" If I had only known! I had done everything just right. I went to the doctor and very proudly explained that we were trying to conceive and that I wanted a checkup to make certain that everything in my body was perfect to house my little miracle. After a general exam, she told me if I had not conceived in six months to call and she would run tests. The first few months the disappointment was mild. I knew it could take a couple of months to conceive, so it was okay that it didn't work the first month. Or the second. By the third, I started to feel a little frustrated but not worried. Month after month passed with no morning sickness, no missed periods, no positive pregnancy test.

Since I had a couple of cousins struggling with infertility, the threat was always in the back of my mind but I didn't really worry about it. My parents had two children beside myself, both of my sisters were able to have children, all of my aunts had children, one set of grandparents had five children, the other set of grandparents had even conceived nine children. Each time the dreaded thought would start to creep into my mind, I would counteract my fear with multiple arguments of the fertility of my family. There were no childless families in my family tree—not even one-child families! We were a fruitful bunch! I couldn't wait to add a branch!

Six months passed and my fear began to grow. In a sense, I still felt I was being a little paranoid getting tests run but I wanted to fix any problem—if there even was one—and start decorating a nursery. I mentioned to my doctor that there were some incidences of polycystic ovarian disease in my family so if she was going to run a bunch of tests she may as well run that one too. I didn't know much about it other than it kept you from getting pregnant.

I anxiously awaited the test results but didn't really expect bad news. The nurse informed me that the results would be back after 1:00 and they would call me then. I was way too impatient for that! I had already waited six months to get pregnant—I certainly wasn't going to wait for their phone call! I went to the office, asked the receptionist to allow me to speak to a nurse to get my test results, and took a seat in the waiting room. I remember the thought running through my head—"The next five minutes will either change my life or will be so insignificant that I won't even remember this day in six months." Little did I know how all consuming that change would be.

The nurse called me back and had me to have a seat in the hallway. This would only take a minute and did not even require putting me in an exam room. She sat down with me and explained the results of my test. "You have polycystic ovarian disease..." Five words carried the weight of the world as they spilled from the nurse's mouth to my ears. I could not process exactly what she meant, but one thing was abundantly, painfully clear. I was infertile. I sat there in the hallway without so much as the four walls of an exam room to hide the destruction of my dreams. I remember nothing beyond the nurse's declaration of the annihilation of the hope of the family I had anticipated my entire life. Everything was in slow motion and I physically felt a tremendous weight pressing down on me. It felt like the air weighed a ton. I know she kept talking. I didn't hear her. I couldn't. I couldn't hear. I couldn't see. I couldn't breathe. But why did it matter? I couldn't have a child.

To all outward appearances, it must have seemed that the news I had just been given didn't matter that much. I thanked the nurse for seeing me and turned stone-faced to walk out of the office. I refused to allow the tears to flow there. The nurse would see no reaction. I walked through the waiting room as though I were a walking dead woman. I walked as quickly as I could through the lobby, through the hospital, into the elevator. No eye contact. No response. The parking garage was only a few hundred feet away. I could hold on. I could make it with no one knowing my world had just ended. However, the realization of the moment began to overwhelm me like a tidal wave and sobs began to spill out of me long before I found asylum within the confines of my vehicle. I felt like I had literally been punched in the stomach and would much rather this had been the truth. I sat there in my car weeping uncontrollably as grief I had never known engulfed every molecule of my being.

After a time, I attempted to gain control of my emotions enough to safely drive my car and headed toward my husband Jason's office. He knew the results came back that day and I knew he was waiting to hear. The drive to his office is non-existent in my memory as it was nothing more than a blur. I do not know how I found my way there other than the mercy of God who must have given His angels charge of my car, gently guiding me though the busy mid-town streets of my city. I'll never forget what it was like to tell my husband that because of me, because of the failure of my body, he may never know the joy of passing his name and his heritage down and extending his family line. He was healthy. I was diseased. He, at the exact moment that I was weeping in the parking garage, was busy in the everyday successes of his job. His world was the same. Mine had crumbled.

I opened the door of his office, numbly stumbled past his secretary and opened his door. I walked in and called his name. His expression changed instantly. How many times does your wife come from a doctor's office with tear stained face and eyes swollen and red before it becomes commonplace? I stood in the doorway and delivered the horrible message that had ripped my heart out and knew I had to throw it at the man who wanted a child as desperately as I. "I have that stupid dis…dis…disease." I literally, physically could not force myself to say the word "disease". I fell into his arms and cried. And cried. And cried. I didn't think I would be able to stop for hours. It had taken all the strength I could muster to hold back the flood waters as I walked through the hospital, but here in the arms of my love, all the strength I had was gone. My tears drenched his shoulder as he stood there in disbelief. Our journey had only just begun.

Our disbelief gave way to determination. We would face this unseen enemy head on. We would see doctors and undergo whatever treatment was necessary to see that our dream became reality. The first thing we knew we had to do was to hit our knees. The first Sunday after I was diagnosed we sought the prayers of our local church. My father was my pastor so he knew immediately what our request was. As is typical for him, my pastor became my Daddy that Sunday as he began to pray. He looked us in the eyes and told us to trust God completely. No matter the outcome—whether God gave us a child or not. Daddy reminded me that God knew the perfect resolution to this problem. Perhaps that was the perfect foundation to build upon as we took our first steps in this journey. I began to weep again and he and my husband wept with me as we began to cry out to God to heal my body and bless my womb. What must the congregation have thought? Here was the choir director, the youth pastor and the senior pastor falling apart in the altar. They didn't know we were grieving the loss of my child and Daddy's grandchild, even though that child had never yet been born, but I felt the strength of their prayers.

I believe that God was deeply and personally involved with my husband and me through every aspect of our struggle. During the early days of our fight, He was there allowing us to grieve. He placed supportive people in our path that understood our pain. God really does work in the most mysterious of ways. Two of the couples closest to us were themselves experiencing infertility and we were able to lean on each other and pray often for each other. No wonder God tells us to bear one another's burden. It's just too heavy to carry alone.

Perhaps most importantly, God truly became the Prince of Peace that He promises to be. I have always been so grateful that He is a God who understands and feels the same pain I feel, but through the incredible pain of infertility this aspect of God became crystal clear to me. Even though I didn't understand what He was doing, and sometimes it felt like my entire world was spinning out of control, I knew He had not forgotten me and that some day all of this would make sense.

Within weeks my medical treatment started. Pills. Shots. Endless blood tests. After a short time of treatment with my regular OBGYN I was referred to an infertility specialist. She told me that she had done all she could do and that I needed the expertise of someone who specialized in my disease. I believe with all my heart that God led us to the doctor who would become so much a part of our lives over the next several months. He and his staff were the most supportive team I could have ever asked for. Their compassion and understanding made this very difficult experience just a little easier to walk through. Whether it was a touch on the shoulder, or spending just a couple of extra minutes to explain what we did not understand, the kindness shown to us as we were hurting and frustrated came like a refreshing cup of water on a hot day. Little did we know that we were impacting the lives of this staff as well.

As the treatment increased, so did the frustrations. The medicines I had to endure were causing "mood swings". In other words—they were turning me into a stark raving lunatic! One moment I would be fine; the next, I'd be bawling my eyes out! My emotions were so crazy that my husband bought me a t-shirt that read "Next mood swing in 6 minutes. Please stand by!" Fortunately, it was on a good day and I thought it was hilarious! Too many days were hard for me, which made it very hard for my husband. Through it all he stood by me and was very patient with me as I bounced off the wall. My tears never seemed to know if it was an appropriate time for them to appear, and they didn't seem to care. I could be standing with friends just talking about our day and, for no reason, the waterworks would begin. One day as I drove into my neighborhood I noticed that the pink clouds looked so pretty against the blue sky. Pink and blue? Oh no! Before I knew what had happened, tears were dripping off of my chin. My poor husband would find me sobbing in the bathroom at 1:00 in the morning because I didn't want to wake him with my heartache. And let's not forget the "Pregnant Woman Magnet" that seems to be placed deep within the barren womb of every infertile woman. Every pregnant woman in our city must have spent untold hours mapping out her day so that some pregnant woman could proudly display her bulging belly to me everywhere I went. Grocery store—there were 2 looking for ripe apples in the produce section. No doubt they want to eat healthy now! Bank—there's a preggie just ahead of me in line. She must have hurried when she saw me getting out of my car! God forbid that I go to the mall—home of hundreds and hundreds of pregnant women. Where did they all come from?

It seemed that everywhere I turned Satan was reminding me that women everywhere were carrying children, some wanted, some unwanted. Some would be loved and taken care of. Others would be abused. Some of these women were thrilled. Some were disgusted. But they were all pregnant. All but me. Daddy had always preached that Satan's primary battleground was your mind. If he could conquer your mind he had you. It sure seemed I was losing the battle. The negative thoughts that were bouncing around my mind seemed to be amplified over loudspeakers a thousand times. "I'll never have a child. Jason could be a father now if only he had married someone else. Why does God withhold this blessing from me and bestow it so freely on others?" The frustration, the negative thoughts, the hopelessness of the situation were almost more than I could bear.

It was at this point that God made my lowest point a turning point in my life. My medicines had been increased, I had undergone two surgeries, countless sonograms, multiple procedures and a diagnosis of another disease, endometriosis. I was struggling to keep my head above water yet determined to hold on to my faith in God. The longer my fight went on, the harder it seemed to keep this faith. Thankfully, God knew just what I needed just when I needed it.

My husband was the youth pastor of the church at the time and he was leading a youth discipleship class. I attended every week, not because I wanted to, but because I felt obligated as his wife to support his ministry. I felt emotionally drained, but I wanted to show my support to him, knowing he had faithfully and lovingly supported me even though he was struggling and hurting as much as I. Part of the course involved homework to be done over the week. I started to work on the week's lesson which required that you spend some time alone thanking God for the ways He shows you He loves you. It was a pretty day outside, so I decided to take a walk and think about God's love. My heart was not in it and I honestly thought I'd just get it over with so I could go on and get my errands taken care of before the day ended. Okay—How did God show me He loved me? I began to thank God for my parents and sisters, their constant love and support, my husband for all he was to me, for the Christian college I was blessed to attend.

All of a sudden God interrupted me! His interruption changed my life forever. ***God spoke to me that day***. A *true, real* message to me. Not in an audible voice, but every bit as real as the audible voice of my husband or anyone else that stands in front of me and speaks to me. It was as real as anything I have ever experienced before. It was specific and I still remember the exact words God spoke to me that day ringing in my mind. His words? "Your infertility is how I show you that I love you."

What? I was so incredibly confused. I decided that if God was going to speak directly to me, I could allow myself to become vulnerable in the precious presence of an Almighty God who loves me deeply. I remember I began to say, "Okay, Lord. You've got to explain this to me because it simply does not make sense to me at all." God asked me a question. "Why do you want a child?" The words poured from my heart as easily as the gallons of tears I had cried. "God, I want to be the one to provide for a child, I want to pick my child up when they fall down and hurt themselves and wipe the hurt away, I want to be the one to run in in the middle of a nightmare and let that child know that everything is okay. I want to be the one to let a child know that they are loved and secure." In that life-changing instant, God ever so gently and lovingly spoke these words to my heart: "That is what I want for you. I want to be the One to provide for you. I want to be the One to pick you up when you've fallen and hurt yourself and wipe your hurt away. I want to be the One to come in the middle of your worst nightmare and let you know that everything is okay. I want to be the One to let you know that you are loved and secure."

Before I could catch my breath, He continued: "You know the pain you feel when you see a pregnant woman and she has what you want, but it just won't seem to come to you? That's how I feel when you won't come to Me." As if that alone wasn't enough to completely remake my understanding of my relationship with God the Father, He continued on. "But the joy you will feel *when your child comes to you* is how I feel when you come to Me."

A million thoughts and emotions flooded over me with a gratitude I cannot begin to describe. God had taken the time and turned His attention to me and the burden I was bearing. It was so real that an eternity of doubt could never diminish my belief in what happened that day. God knew exactly what to speak to my heart. In only an instant He turned the greatest sorrow of my life into my greatest blessing! God loved me! God desired me! I had heard it all my life, I had known it and absolutely believed it. But this day, this knowledge became more real to me than at any other time in my life. He used the hurt and agony of infertility to show me how much I mean to Him! No wonder He calls Himself Abba Father! He is a parent longing for His child, just as I was longing for a child of my own! When I couldn't hold my child in my arms, He understood because there were far too many times that I wouldn't let Him hold me in His. No sermon, no Sunday school lesson, no Bible study could have ever taught me in 10,000 years what God taught me in only a few seconds. What a blessing my infertility had become!

Not only did healing begin in that instant, but also at that moment in my life, I knew I would have a child! God said, "When your child comes to you..." The Giver of Life was telling me I would be a mother. No pregnancy test could ever be more confirming than what God did for me that day! That confirmation of my miracle would sustain me through more confusing months and difficult medical treatment.

After this promise from God, my outlook changed. Yes, the hard times were still there. Yes, the tears still fell. Yes, the frustration continued to creep up. It was still difficult to see very pregnant women parading their swollen figures everywhere I went, but now they were reminders to me that God desired me! Every time I began to feel weak and tired of this seemingly everlasting trial, I would remind myself that God had spoken and just like Abraham and Sarah we waited on the promise of God to become manifest in the form of a child.

On March 21, 1999 I received the news I had begged God for throughout most of my marriage. A pregnancy was confirmed! God's promised child was on its way! Even before her birth, this child was touching people for God! Those who had petitioned God on our behalf were witness to the miracle of new life, given by the Giver of Life. Through our story many were reminded that God had answered the petition for a child and He was to receive the glory no matter man's efforts. She was going to be the fulfillment of God's promise in the flesh! A miracle I could touch and hold!

Throughout the next nine months there were as many tears as there were throughout my battle with infertility, only this time they were tears of joy! God had blessed us beyond measure and on November 29, 1999 Alexis Noelle Forbus was placed in my arms. Indescribable joy and gratitude flooded my heart in ways that are beyond words. God's blessings to me of infertility and fertility were almost more than I am able to comprehend even now.

Throughout my struggle, I was blessed to sense God's presence in a way that I would not have been able to without infertility. I would never have believed that God could use the hurt of barren-ness so and bring me to a point to where I would look you in the face and say without hesitation that my infertility was—and is—a blessing. I have learned lessons throughout the whole process that I never could have learned any other way. I thank God that He used this to reach me, teach me and change me. It is my prayer that God will use your battle to bring victory to your life and to the lives of those you touch.

Things to remember about Jason & Beth's story:

> Your mind is the primary battleground Satan uses to defeat you.
> God can use your infertility to show you how much He loves you.
> God can use your hurt to bring you closer to Him.
> Your struggle can simply be a road map leading you to ministry.

Adoption
Ordered Steps

Perhaps one of the most difficult areas of the infertility saga is knowing when enough is enough. We'll do almost anything to have that long sought after pregnancy. If someone told us that if we would stand on our heads in the corner of the room for seven hours straight wearing one purple sock and one orange sock that it would increase our chances of pregnancy, we would do it even if it we thought it was absolutely ridiculous! We try. It doesn't work. We try again. It still doesn't work. Over and over and over and over—we truly are the triumph of hope over experience!

For many of us, difficult treatment or the monthly struggle is nothing compared to the heart-wrenching decision to stop trying. But your body says "enough". Your bank account says "enough". Your spouse says "enough". Your doctor says "enough". Your heart simply says, "I cannot take it anymore". The dream of a blissful, joyous pregnancy has come crashing to an end. However, the decision to end the quest for a biological child does not mean that you may never have a child. Adoption is such a wonderful, loving choice and has turned many a quiet room into a beautifully noisy nursery! To take a child from a life of nothingness and fill it with love, compassion and family is a wonderful, noble thing!

Adoption is not failure. If you come to the point that it is physically impossible to conceive, financially irresponsible, or just simply too hard emotionally to continue to hope and have those hopes dashed every month, you have choices to make. Once the door has closed on having a biological child you now face the challenge of choosing adoption or choosing to live your life childless. Neither is a failure and both can be blessed, happy lives. Sometimes we have to decide if we want to be pregnant or if we want to be parents. If pregnancy itself is not a driving force, adoption can be a real lifesaver for you and for a precious child who has for whatever reason been denied its own biological family.

What does the Bible say about adoption? It says many wonderful things! First of all, as Christians we are all adopted! Romans says that we are adopted as sons and cry "Abba Father!" "Abba" literally translated is "Daddy". This causes us to realize a deep intimate relationship between Father and child. Not an absent or uncaring parent who brings us into existence and is finished with us—but Daddy! The loving, laughing, teaching parent that a Daddy is. In fact the Scripture continues and calls us sons. It goes even further and says if we are sons, then heirs and joint heirs with Jesus! As an adopted child of God we are co-equal with Jesus in God's eyes! He loves us equally with Jesus! We are as worthy as Jesus in God's eyes! We are just as precious, just as desirous, and He longs for our companionship just as much as He does Jesus'!

So what does that say about the adopted child? Unfortunately, there are those who feel that adoption is a choice only to be made when everything else fails and "this will just have to do". It comes across as if adoption is second best and the adopted child somehow does not measure up to a child born of your own body. Nothing could be further from the truth! We are held just as dear as Jesus Christ Himself in the heart of our loving Heavenly Father! What a beautiful, undeniable comparison of the biological and the adopted child! God loved His own begotten Son and called us co-heirs with Him! An adopted child is no less precious, no less valuable, and no less a blessing than a biological child. A child need not come from your womb to take residence deep inside your heart. I believe God has a special blessing for the man and woman who open their hearts and their homes to a child not born of their bodies but of their hearts.

As I have mentioned before, some of our very dearest friends were experiencing infertility at the same time my husband and I were traveling this road. After years of trying to conceive to no avail, these precious friends of ours chose adoption. After deciding to pursue a child through international adoption, the adoption agency was contacted and they began to fulfill the necessary requirements to bring a Russian child into their family. Throughout the endless mounds of paperwork only to be followed by more endless mounds of paperwork an amazing thing happened. Both the man and the woman fell hopelessly in love with an unknown, unspecified child in a land thousands of miles away. Not only had they never held this child or seen it's face, a specific child had not been assigned to them. They never even knew if the child was a boy or a girl or if the child had yet been born. However, both man and woman miraculously became parents in their hearts sometime during the process.

Due to unfortunate circumstances within the adoption agency, the long awaited adoption fell through. For this couple, it was much like a miscarriage. The child they hoped for, waited for and longed for was not to be a part of their family. God moved in a mighty way throughout this era of their lives and although the adoption was not to be, a short time after the failed adoption, she became pregnant. Boy, did she become pregnant! They are now the parents of healthy, happy triplets—two boys and a girl! Their home is happier—and louder—than they ever could have dreamed!

The point of this illustration? It's certainly not to depress you with a sad story. To discourage you from trying to adopt? Not at all. The part of the story I want to emphasize is what the mother told me while she was pregnant with her triplets. As we were talking after church one Sunday night, we were discussing our own struggles with infertility, how God had worked in incredible ways throughout our battles when the subject of her adoption came up. With her hand on her growing tummy, she began to tell her emotional view of the child she thought she would adopt. She described how although she never met him or her, never knew the child's gender, she loved that child passionately. The fact that God opened her womb and blessed her more than she ever dreamed never lessened her love for the child she planned to adopt. The love for the adopted child was there as she described a real connection to a child in Russia. I'm so thrilled for her that she has conceived and has a beautiful, large family. And I think it's really interesting that the subject of adoption is not closed for them—even with their triplets!

I believe that God gives certain understanding through circumstances. The couple that has chosen to adopt, has completed their dossier, paid all the fees and passed all the inspections stands ready and anxious for the day the child can be brought into their home. The nursery is ready, for they have gone and prepared a place for their child. Their hearts are bursting with love for a child who as of yet doesn't love them back, and has nothing to give in return—no valuables, no great life experience, no great wisdom. Just being *their child* gives that child its unfathomable worth! The parents have paid all that had to be paid and made every sacrifice necessary for that child to take the family name and its rightful place at their table.

Never once was the adopted child expected to carry his weight in the adoption process. The child couldn't! How ludicrous it would be to demand that the tiny orphan be responsible for all documents being properly notarized and signed by the right people, that the child provide the necessary finances and turn everything in in a timely manner! This child doesn't have the physical or mental ability or the provisions. And how much more ridiculous to assume that the parents refuse to act on the child's behalf until he or she becomes able to fulfill the necessary requirements. No, you'll never hear an awaiting adoptive mother call the adoption agency and say, "Well, if that baby is not smart enough to fill out those forms we'll just wait until he is!" No! The wait for a child is excruciating at best!

So, the child is unable to provide for himself. No ability of his own. No influence with important people. No favors to call in. Just existing in a state of need. The hardship increases a little every single day. Disaster? Not at all. The adoptive parent has the ability, the provision and most importantly, the desire to do for that child what the child cannot do for himself. All the child needs to be is their child. They will see that all will be done to allow this child a forever family.

They tell their friends about this child. They dream. They get excited talking about this child. (Have you ever noticed the twinkle in the eye of the parent waiting to adopt? It's amazingly similar to the twinkle in the eye of the pregnant woman!) Now they wait with almost unbearable anticipation for the sound of the phone to ring and the voice on the line say "Come get your child!" The absolute perfected joy when parent and child are united! Not for a few hours or a few days but from now on! No separation! The child living in the presence of the parent so in love that they would rather die than live without this precious child!

Can't you see the parallel between earthly and spiritual adoption? A loving parent longing for communion with a child provides for that child to be forever adopted into His family. He gives that child His Name, His provision, His protection and most of all—His infinite love! I don't think anyone understands God's longing for us to join Him in Heaven like an adoptive parent waiting for their child to come to them. He has made all the provision necessary. Every price has been paid. He has done for you what you could not do for yourself. He loves His child with an unspeakable passion. He has sacrificed. He's made His home ready. He surely tells the heavenly host all about you! After all—He knows everything there is to know about you! He has certainly proven that He would rather die than live without you—that's just what He did! And He's waiting with nearly unbearable anticipation for His child to come home—He's simply waiting to give the word for Gabriel to give the call— "Come home! Your Father's ready and waiting for you!"

Perhaps one of the most exciting aspects of the preparation to adopt is choosing a new name for the child. The parents try this name, then that one. Over and over again they search books and ask opinions. Little by little the list is whittled down until the perfect name is chosen. One thing, however, requires no debate, no questioning. When the papers are signed and the child is perfectly placed within the new family, the child is given the family name and all the rights and privileges that go along with it. Anyone who hears the child's name will know exactly who they belong to! The rights of the family name? How precious they are! A permanent place in the family home, loving protection by people who adore you and have promised to be there forever, the blessed knowledge that you are welcome in their presence.

When we become a child of God, we are given His Name—we are known as Christians! What a wonderful name to bear! With this Name we can expect God's provision and protection. We are welcomed into His glorious presence! All because we are adopted into His family and called by His Name!

One night when my daughter was 2 years old, we were spending the night at my parents' home. She had not felt well, so she was sleeping with me. At about 4 A.M., I was awakened by a violent shaking. In the first groggy moments, I didn't know if we were having an earthquake or if I was just having a very real dream. This dream quickly turned into a horrendous nightmare as I realized my child was having a seizure. Terror I had never known gripped me as tightly as I gripped my convulsing baby. As her eyes rolled back in her head and her body thrashed in my arms, my husband and I made a mad dash to my parents' bedroom. We needed them to pray and we needed them to pray *now!*

What do you think I did when I reached their bedroom door? Do you think I stood there with my sick child and discussed with my husband whether or not I should wake them up? Did we debate whether we should talk to them or someone else down the road? Did we go back to our room and wait for a more convenient time or place? How many times do you think I knocked? At that moment of need I didn't wait, I didn't wonder. I burst through the door and screamed "Daddy! Lexie's having a seizure! Pray!!!"

That's when Daddy rolled over in bed and said "Okay, in the morning. First thing." Right? No! Instantly, in the middle of the night he and Mother were on their feet pleading the blood of Jesus over my child. They never fussed at me for coming in uninvited or unannounced. They did not tell me to come back later. When they realized their child and their grandchild had a crisis and needed them, nothing else mattered. They immediately responded to my need.

What made us the focus of their attention that night? I was their child and my daughter was their grandchild. Nothing else mattered. Not my education, not my worth to the world. Any riches I had carried no weight at all. All that mattered was that I carried their name. When we are adopted children of God, He tells us to boldly approach His throne to find help in the time of need. All we need is His Name. He'll move Heaven and earth if the need be to take care of His own. As the adopted child of God, we cry "Abba!"—"Daddy!" and we have the attention of Heaven. We need no invitation. We need no escort. All we need is His Name.

Hurting? Burst through His door! Scared? He's there to comfort you. Confused as to what path you should take on your journey toward parenthood? He's all-knowing and all in love with you! Your Abba Father—"Daddy"—anxiously awaits communion with you, His precious, much loved and desired adopted child.

So, is adoption a failure in your battle with infertility? Absolutely not! Perhaps you've gone down a different path than you intended at the beginning, but remember Proverbs 3:5-6:

"Trust in the Lord with all your heart and do not lean on your own understanding. In all your ways acknowledge Him, and He will make your paths straight."

Psalm 37:23 tells us that the steps of a good man are ordered by the Lord and He even delights in your way. He will order your steps down the path that He knows in His divine, ultimate wisdom is best for you. He rejoices with you when you follow His path. How wonderful to know that God will celebrate with you as you adopt the child He has prepared for you!

Have you trusted Him? Chances are you have had to trust Him more since your infertility story began than you ever have in your entire life. Has your experience been too hard for you to understand? How comforting and how blessed it is that we don't have to—and are even told not to—lean on our own understanding. We are able to lean on His understanding when ours is simply not clear enough. Have you acknowledged Him? Asked Him what to do? Before each decision, have you dropped to your knees, bowed your head and submissively asked His divine guidance in this quest? Then He has directed your path! If you fulfill His requirements, the promise is more sure than money in the bank. Trust. Acknowledge. He will direct your paths. If Christ directed your path to this child, how could you possibly call the adoption of this child a failure?

Things to remember about adoption:

> ➤ The adoption of a child into the specific family God has chosen is no less a miracle than the miracle of birth.
> ➤ We are adopted children of God.
> ➤ We are joint-heirs with Christ.
> ➤ Just as an adopted child carries your name, we carry God's Name.
> ➤ Our steps leading to adoption are ordered by God.

Child Loss
King David's Story

*Then the Lord struck the child that Uriah's widow bore to David,
so that he was very sick. David therefore inquired of God for the
child; and David fasted and went and lay all night on the ground.
The elders of his household stood beside him in order to raise him
up from the ground, but he was unwilling and would not eat food
with them. Then it happened on the seventh day that the child died.
And the servants of David were afraid to tell him that the child was
dead, for they said, "Behold, while the child was still alive, we
spoke to him and he did not listen to our voice. How then can we
tell him that the child is dead, since he might do himself harm!"
But when David saw that his servants were whispering together,
David perceived that the child was dead; so David said to his
servants, "Is the child dead?" And they said "He is dead." So
David arose from the ground, washed and anointed himself, and
changed his clothes; and he came into the house of the Lord and
worshiped. Then he came to his own house, and when he
requested, they set food before him and he ate. Then his servants
said to him, "What is this thing that you have done? While the
child was alive, you fasted and wept; but when the child died, you
arose and ate food." He said, "While the child was still alive, I
fasted and wept; for I said 'Who knows, the Lord may be gracious
to me, that the child may live.' "But now he has died; why should I
fast? Can I bring him back again? I will go to him,
but he will not return to me."*
2 Samuel 12:16-23

Throughout the pages of the Bible, we see men and women just like us with the same emotions, joys and sorrows we each experience. Although the day-to-day life was different—I don't think any of you rode camels to get to work this morning—people have been the same for centuries. We love our families, we laugh, we cry, and from the beginning of time until the end of eternity, we all need God.

David was no different from you or me in many ways. Although he was a mighty King, he had to live through a great sorrow that some of you reading these words have had to survive: the death of his child.

According to Scripture, David and Bathsheba entered into a sinful relationship that produced a son. No matter the foundation of their relationship, just like people today, one look at that tiny infant in his arms and surely his heart felt like it was going to melt and run out the ends of his toes! David loved this child passionately just like people today love their children.

The Bible tells us that David pleaded with God for the child. This doesn't imply a passive, "Okay, God, um, if it's okay, don't let the kid die. That'd be nice. Thanks." On the contrary, he begged, he pleaded. We are told that he spent the nights lying on the ground and refused to even eat. His servants didn't know what to do. They gathered around him and tried to make him get up and get something to eat. It didn't matter. David's heart was slowly being broken into. For seven days he begged God and I believe he did nothing else. The man was totally devastated. He did all he knew to do to save this child's life. Imagine this scene; the great King of Israel reduced to a sobbing, pitiful pile of humanity all because of the love of a child! Lying face down, broken, begging God for the life of his baby. No longer the majestic powerful King who received anything he desired by simply saying the word. Used to having whatever servant with whatever talent was necessary to do his bidding, David now lay helpless and shattered petitioning God to spare his son.

Eyes swollen and face tearstained, tears streaming into puddles on the floor, David no doubt felt his world was coming to an end. Helpless, scared, grief-stricken. Was any price too high for the salvation of this tiny infant? Abdicate the throne? In a heartbeat!

Give up his own life? Without one moment's hesitation! David, however, was not given these options. He had to walk through the next very painful stage of his existence.

After seven days of heart wrenching pleading and begging with an unseen God, the baby succumbed to illness and went into eternity. When the servants realized the boy died, they were afraid to even tell David. Why? They were afraid he would hurt himself. Somehow, though shrouded in grief, David knew his baby had died. He saw the servants whispering among themselves and turning his tear-stained face towards theirs, asked the dreaded question; "Is the child dead?" Nothing could be said but "He is dead." There was nothing more to be said.

Some women sense something is wrong with their pregnancy. Terrified, they see the doctor and hear those horrible words—"I can't find a heartbeat." Others tip-toe into quiet nurseries expecting to find a peacefully slumbering infant. Instead they find that their precious child has succumbed to SIDS. The sinking feeling, the all-consuming dread and fear. All soon gives way to an unbelievable, crushing grief. Family and friends often don't know what to say. Words cannot ease the pain anyway. David's servants were speechless, as well. If your heart has known this indescribable pain, please, blink back your tears enough to see the picture of this once mighty man literally knocked flat on the floor and know there is a brother sharing your pain in King David.

Perhaps you've experienced the massive mind numbing devastation only brought about by the death of your child. Your sorrow is unequaled by any tragedy known to mankind. Have you been there? Change the name, change the scenery and you may see yourself in this scenario. If so, hang on. Before now, you simply could not imagine how one so small, perhaps even unseen by human eye, and to the world so insignificant, could become the total focus of your life, your thoughts, your emotions. One little person so tiny creates a wound in your heart so great, so overwhelming that you feel you'll never recover. Many people living with grief find themselves abandoned by friends. Families feel awkward and tend to talk about everything else but the baby you've loved and lost. If so, you must feel like King David felt.

King David has wept. He has refused to eat. No doubt sleep has escaped him. After all, pillows drenched with tears aren't conducive to sleep. But look now at what David did. The Bible does not say, "David was useless from this day on." It does not say, "After the death of his child, David's life was without joy." Absent also in this story is David dying along with his child. Read verse 20:

> *"So David arose from the ground, washed, anointed himself and changed his clothes; and he came into the house of the Lord and worshiped."*

He did what? He **_worshiped!_** How could he do this? He begged God to spare the life of his child, God could have but He chose not to. He was the giver of life—He could have simply said the word and the breath of life would have surged through that baby's lungs once again. Yet, David immediately **_chose_** to worship. "But my heart hurts too much to worship!" Was David's heart not broken? Sure it was! But he made the conscious choice to worship God. Perhaps this was the time he penned those blessed, God-breathed words, "Even though I walk through the valley of the shadow of death, I fear no evil, for You are with me." Surely he worshiped through tears. In the face of death and tragedy, tears are a constant companion. So how could he worship? He worshiped because he knew God is a good God! God is sovereign and God is just! Even if his emotions were screaming at him to turn his back on God and forget a God who refused to help a tiny baby, something deep inside David knew that our emotions don't always understand truth, and the truth was God still loved David and had a plan for his life anyway.

After David worshiped, he went home and ate. I'm sure that to his servants this seemed unreal. He nearly grieved himself to death yet now he simply returned to everyday life? How dare he? How dare you go back to work and church so quickly? Why are you teaching that Sunday School class now? Why not give up for a while? How dare my spouse expect me to act as if nothing happened? How can you go on? How can you live? How can you expect me to?

David's servants, confidants and probably even his wife wondered the same. They questioned him as though he was crazy because he was picking up the pieces of his broken heart so soon after his loss. "Why are you acting this way?" Look at David's responses to his servants in verses 22-23. "I wept, I fasted, I did all I could do. My child died. This is not what I wanted. This is not what I begged God for!" But David's discourse doesn't end here! "Can I bring him back again? No! I would if I could but that is not the case!" But—a light begins to shine through his grief and in our mind's eye we can start to see some of that same determination in David's eyes as the bear and the lion must've seen in the moments before their demise. The look that comes from knowing deep down inside that victory is coming! The same look of confidence that turned Goliath's arrogance and ridicule into realization of defeat! Oh, the death of his baby was a greater challenge than any he had faced before, yet somehow David knew that it was not the end for him. David simply says, "I will go to him!"

What glorious comfort! David knew that he would once again hold this child, look into his eyes, hear his giggle, tousle his hair! This gave David the strength he needed to survive such a loss. But wait! Do you realize the massive significance of this statement? David lived in the Old Testament days. Jesus had not yet been born. The cross and the resurrection were centuries away. Jesus had yet to stand face to face with death, hell and the grave and conquer them forever. No one had heard or recorded those precious words "I go to prepare a place for you". Nor had John penned the words—"he who believes in Me will live even if he dies." How did David know? Perhaps God quietly spoke peace to his heart—"You'll see him again." Listen as God whispers to you through your grief: "Your child is with Me, safe, content, waiting for you. I'll hold him for you until you get here."

A dear friend of mine was a kindergarten teacher and was unusually gifted with children. They seemed to be drawn to her and she to them. After years of trying, she and her husband conceived and she had a totally normal pregnancy until she was about five months along. They suffered a devastating miscarriage and lost their little boy.

Through the many stages of their grief, my friend described a loss unique to her situation. As a teacher, she thrilled each time a child experienced the joy of learning, their eyes lighting up with recognition. She had so looked forward to teaching her child his numbers, his colors, his letters. When autumn rolled around and school supplies stocked the store shelves, this loss again seemed so great. No child to teach, no willing student to learn at her knee. However, like David, God knew just when and how to give the perfect gift to bring peace and healing.

One night as she was sleeping, my friend began to dream. In her dream she saw a child and knew it was the baby she had lost. She saw her little boy snuggled in the lap of Jesus as they sat in the middle of a field. Jesus would play with the boy, call him Jacob (which was the name given to the child during the pregnancy) and both were laughing and at ease. Jacob would ask Jesus questions. "What's this, Jesus?" Jesus would answer, "That's a butterfly, Jacob." "What's this?" "Well, Jacob, that flower's called a dandelion." After many questions, answers and loving interactions, my friend said that Jesus turned His attention to her and it seemed that He was looking outside of the dream and straight into her hurt. He stared directly at her as He spoke and His words pierced her heart and brought healing to the wounds suffered through her loss. "Jacob is learning creation from the Creator."

God knew her specific hurt and He knew the balm needed to soothe the pain. That particular dream may not have been as healing to another but it was so perfect for her. God spoke healing directly to her heart. What a wonderful, loving Father we have. He knows us, loves us, grieves with us and provides healing for wounds so great that only divine intervention can suffice. The healing is yours. It may take time and tears, but it is no mistake that Christ is called the Great Physician. But how can He know the grief I feel? Find comfort in the fact that He knows specifically how you feel, for you see, His child died, too.

God knows firsthand the grief of a parent whose heart has been crushed by a child's death. He stood heavyhearted on the precipice of Glory and watched as His Child bled and died. No doubt that God, whose emotions are millions upon millions of times deeper than our own, wept millions of times more tears than we could. Imagine your grief multiplied literally ten's of millions of times and maybe you can begin to understand the depth of God's grief.

What does this mean? It means you can pour out your heart to Him and He'll understand. When friends and family and even your spouse can't bear to see your tears anymore, God has incredibly broad shoulders for you to cry on and strong arms for you to fall into. Lay your head on His chest and hear His heart beating. A heart that broke, just like yours .

As you find comfort in the bosom of Love Himself, don't forget to look into His eyes and see the promise of a heavenly and eternal reunion with your child. One that will not end in miscarriage. No SIDS allowed inside the gates of pearl! No stilled heartbeats. No blighted ovums. No spontaneous abortions. No grief. No sadness. Just an eternity with the child you've held in your heart so much longer than in your body! And an eternity with a God who loved you enough to orchestrate the death of His only Son to provide a way to reunite you with your child.

When rewards are passed out in Heaven, I'm sure there will be missionaries, martyrs, ministers and precious saints of God lining those golden avenues and their rewards will be so great that nothing on earth could ever begin to compare. Those who have sacrificed so much to lead so many to this place of eternal joy and reconciliation and worship of a loving Heavenly Father no doubt deserve more than the grandest wealth of all time. However, although this is just my imagination and my opinion, I would love to see the scene that I imagine unfolding when you get home.

You've just entered the joy of Heaven and you're absolutely amazed and dumbfounded. Never in your wildest imaginations could you have envisioned such a place of joy and perfection. Suddenly you feel an incredible holiness as you turn and see God the Father coming *straight for you*. You feel such a sense of awe at the very sight of Him! The angels even step aside to make a path from Him to you and you notice that even they are beginning to smile. They know what's coming! Suddenly, you realize that He comes bearing a precious gift. What is it? It's not a crown to wear. Not a record of your good works. No, this gift is kicking and squirming, softly cooing and so very much alive! The stilled fingers you once tearfully counted are now squirming and reaching to touch your face! The little eyes, once closed in death are sparking and twinkling and are the absolute most beautiful shade of blue you've ever seen!

I pray that you will receive as the first of your rewards, the most precious thing life on earth had to offer—the child you lost. All the sorrow of earth will fade in the joy of this moment! Psalm 127 tells us that children are a gift and a reward. Your gift is unopened, waiting for your arrival. Do whatever you can to make it to heaven! All you have to do is accept His salvation and with a joyful, redeemed heart join Him at His home. He—and your child—are waiting for you there.

As you journey through your grief there are things you can do to help yourself. Learn from the example of David. Choose to worship God. It may be a difficult choice but one that will be very healing. Be patient with yourself as you heal. You didn't dream of and fall in love with this child overnight; the hurt won't go away overnight either. Allow yourself the luxury of walking through the grief process.

Following a loss of a baby, many couples try to find meaning in their loss. For some, the meaning is crystal clear. For others, it may be less apparent. Whatever the case, one thing is sure; God can use this ordeal for your good and for His glory! Romans 8:28 says that God causes all things to work together for good to those who love God, to those who are called according to His purpose. Does that mean that the loss of your precious baby is good? Is it good that your heart feels as if it is being physically ripped from your chest? No. That's not what that verse says or means. It does say that if you love God and are called according to His purpose that He can take a tragedy even this great and work it for your good. What an amazing God of paradoxes we serve! He takes the worst experience life can throw at you and He works it for good. No one else can do for you what God can!

You may never know the reason for your loss until you are able to stand face to face with your Heavenly Father as He lovingly shows you the plan He masterfully orchestrated in your life. One couple experiencing the loss of a baby to an ectopic pregnancy after a decade of infertility exhibited such a beautiful example of trusting

God in the midst of their heartache. Their church family reached out to them to hold them up when the baby was lost, but instead the couple ministered to everyone at the church. Their testimony rang loud and clear that they trusted God totally and were even in regular church services within three days of their loss!

Had it not been for this lost baby, the mother would never have discovered two different medical conditions she had. Had it not been for the baby she lost, she would not be the mother of her three beautiful children she conceived shortly after her loss! Both husband and wife truly believe God used this baby to accomplish miracles in their lives. This child accomplished in only eight short weeks every single thing God had laid out for his or her life! I haven't done that in over 35 years! Do you see how this beautiful testimony is so much more healing than allowing Satan to convince you that God doesn't care or that He is out of control?

Whether or not God chooses to reveal His perfect plan to you this side of eternity, He has never turned away a hurting child—it's simply not in His character. He will lovingly guide you through if you'll allow Him. There is no doubt that your trial will present opportunities for you to minister to others. What a great blessing to come from such heartache! 2 Corinthians 1:3 tells us to comfort one another with the same comfort we receive from God. It also tells us that through Christ our comfort will overflow! Who understands the loss of a baby better than someone who has already walked the same road!

If you do lose a child, try to find some way to memorialize this life. People who have never experienced the loss of an unborn or stillborn child tend to view the baby as an "it", not a child. One grieving mother said she had no place to put flowers on anniversaries or holidays, so she and her husband built a beautiful fountain in their yard to memorialize the life of their son. Find a way—plant a tree, release balloons on special days, talk to your pastor about beginning a memorial service for lost babies. It will be therapeutic for you and your family and serve to honor to the life of your child for years to come

Things to remember about David's story:

> ➤ David loved deeply and grieved deeply.
> ➤ David *chose* to worship.
> ➤ David's life continued and was prosperous after the death of his child.
> ➤ If you're a Christian, you will be reunited with your child.
> ➤ Find a way to memorialize the life of the child you've lost.

Rivers & Mountains

The struggle with infertility is so hard, and at times, it feels totally overwhelming. I seem to think better in pictures than in words so let me describe it to you this way.

Infertility can be seen much like a river in front of you. On the surface it is calm, steady, cool and refreshing. You stand on the banks and look across the waters, ready to make the journey, for on the other side is the fulfillment of your dreams. A life of peace and contentment, a feeling of completion and happiness. All you have to do is get there—cross the river. So many people make this journey effortlessly. Surely your endeavor will prove to be the same. You've prepared and you've prayed. You're ready to make the trip to the other side of the river. You never dreamed you'd have a problem.

The journey begins! Excitement melds with the curiosity of what lies ahead. You tread into the water that looks so calm, but beneath the surface there is so much more than meets the eye. Rocks hidden beneath that you didn't expect turn your ankle and cause you to fall and get hurt. You didn't expect to get hurt—you were just traveling to the other side of this river. That's okay—you pick yourself up and try again. Once again you set your face toward the other side and take the next step. Suddenly you find you're caught in a current, strong and powerful. The current is so mighty that it pulls you down time after time after time. You simply cannot fight this unseen enemy—it's so much stronger than you. It looks so peaceful on the surface, but the undercurrent is lurking beneath. Just when you think you're strong enough to try to move on, you go down again, this time totally immersed in the waters. You come up sputtering and gasping for breath—drowning in a river of frustration, sorrow, hurt, misunderstanding.

You notice too, that the river is so much wider now than when you began. It started out really as just a stream—a few steps to make and you'd be there. All of a sudden, this looks like the Mississippi River at it's widest and wildest point. How in the world will you ever make it across?

You find yourself back at your starting point. You stand and gaze longingly at the other side while so many around you easily travel from point A to point B. Some are happy, some act as though they don't even realize how they got there or where they're going. Some turn to you as they sail past you and tell you to relax—you're fighting the river too hard. Others tell you how much more beautiful this side of the river is than the other. Nothing matters. You've tried your best. Yet here you stand. Right where you started. For you, this river is just simply uncrossable.

Perhaps infertility has been the huge mountain looming in your path. From a distance, it is so beautiful. Haven't you ever gazed on a mountain rising majestically on the horizon and think to yourself that you'd love to conquer it? Quite the lofty goal! But somehow, as you get closer, you notice things that you might not have seen had you kept your distance. After all, the closer you get, the higher the mountain looms. You find things you never imagined. Things like the skinny, winding, treacherous paths leading around the mountain, the steep terrain.

Every step is difficult, sometimes dangerous. If you can find a trail it's narrow, rocky, scary. You find that as you try to climb this mountain you lose your step time after time, and you find yourself back at the very bottom. But you're determined. Time after time you reach for the pinnacle, that high and lofty goal. However, you never can seem to find that sure footing. You feel the very ground beneath you slide away. You climb up one step and slide back down. The goal is always just out of reach.

What seemed so peaceful and beautiful has now become hard,

frustrating and cold. People go to mountains to relax; yet it's become a symbol of your struggle. You can't go around it—it's just too wide. You sure can't go over it—you've tried everything you can and it's just too high. You can't go under it—the weight would no doubt crush you. And you cannot tunnel through it. It's just too hard and too strong. So you find yourself in the valley. This lonesome valley. Others have made it. Why can't you?

Just like the analogy of the river, the quest to have a child at first seemed exciting and no doubt, many of us made the announcement with pride—"We're trying to have a baby!" However, before long, there were rocks and currents to surprise us. Of course, we keep struggling, keep trying. One more month. One more round of tests. Before long, you find that the current is overwhelming and you've been pulled under. How many more doctor's appointments or friend's baby showers can you attend? You find yourself drowning in a river of despair and misunderstanding.

Or perhaps you can relate to the mountain story. Perhaps you've come close to attaining the goal of a big family only to hear the doctor say those terrible, dreaded words, "I'm sorry," and you find yourself back at the base of the mountain. You lose your footing each time a new disease is diagnosed or a medical answer cannot be found. You climb one side only to fall off the cliff when you learn that the adoption has fallen through—again.

If these stories describe how you have felt as you have so courageously fought this most difficult of battles, I invite you to sing with me the words of an old hymn written so many years ago:

> *Got any rivers you think are uncrossable?*
> *Got any mountains you can't tunnel through?*
> *God specializes in things thought impossible!*
> *And He'll do for you what no other power can do!*

We serve a powerful God, more powerful than any river or mountain in your way. Remember, God is the all-powerful creator of Heaven and Earth and He created all the mountains and rivers on the entire planet. If need be, He can recreate those mountains and rivers and move them from your way.

Everyone reading these words is doing so because an unforeseen mountain or river placed itself in your path. It has caused hurts and fears you never could have imagined if you had not had trouble achieving what so many easily do and some even by accident. Some have struggled for years and years and others are just beginning the journey. For all of us, I want to share just a couple of Scriptures that have really ministered to me.

In the stories of the births of Isaac and Jesus Himself we see some similarities. Astonished parents. Surprise. A promised child. But I want to point out to you a couple of very similar and wonderful statements undoubtedly proclaimed with a twinkle in the eye of the holy messenger who was honored to share it. Go back with me to Sarah's tent as the angel of the Lord told her at the tender young age of 89 that within one year she would finally bear the child she had craved her entire life. What was that blessed question to the dazed octogenarian? "Is anything too difficult for the Lord?" (Genesis 18:14) I know she laughed but I can't help but think that the angel had to at least snicker at her expression!

Now jump ahead to the central event of mankind—the birth of Christ. Look with me as a scared young girl stares an angel in the face as he tells her she is carrying the Lamb of God in her virgin womb. What was his message to this confused young girl? "For nothing will be impossible with God!" (Luke 1:37)

See any similarities? Both of these statements were uttered to reassure the mothers of children who otherwise could not have been born! It took a miracle to breathe life into the womb of a 90-year-old woman and even more miracle working power to bring the Son of God into the human body of a virgin teenager! I absolutely love that God placed those two Scriptures boldly screaming out through time and eternity that nothing is too difficult for God right smack dab in the middle of the accounts of these children! Both statements were uttered in response to the conception of children! That really speaks to me as a woman who has felt the sting of childlessness myself!

Let me tattoo this on your heart right now—Nothing is too hard for God! Nothing! Hallelujah! Endometriosis? It's nothing to the Great Physician! Unexplained infertility? Not to an all-knowing God! Miscarriages? Stillbirths? God understands—remember He knows the sting of losing a Child. His child died, too. Adoption? He is the original adoptive parent!

Nothing, nothing, absolutely nothing is too difficult for God and He's fighting this battle right along with you! Disease? He can heal! Financially strapped? His very Name—Jehovah Jireh—proclaims to you that He is your Provider! Confused? He can lead you to the right doctors or support groups! Tired? He can give you rest! Barren? He can open your womb! We serve such a wonderful God. I'm so glad He loves me and cares about my hurt!

In John 10:10, Christ states "I am come that they might have life, and that they might have it more abundantly" (KJV). Not just life, although that in and of itself would be a miraculous blessing! But **_abundant_** life! Life to the fullest extent possible endowed by the very Creator of life! If we are His children, if we are joint-heirs with Christ—and we know we are because we are assured this in Scripture—what in this world makes you think He wants us feeling unfulfilled, unloved and lonely?

It would be wonderful enough if Christ said **_abundant_** life. But, notice the next to the last word—**_more_**. Not just barely enough, not even enough, but life **_more_** abundantly. If you had to describe what an abundant life was, what would you say? Christ came into this world to give you an abundant life, but then He stops as if to say that even that is not good enough for His child. He wants us to have life **_more abundantly_**!

Sometimes the hardest thing for us to accept is that not everyone who desires a child and tries to have children actually has children. Some of us may never conceive a child of our own. Some of us will live the remainder of our lives childless; some through choice, some not by choice. Those of us who have been consumed with baby hunger are really incredible people. You have stared medical science and your fertile friends and relatives in the face and said, "I will succeed!" You have stood toe to toe with heartache and you continue to fight with the bravery of a mighty warrior. But for some, there comes a time to lay down your weapons and rest in the arms of a Savior who loves you and who truly understands baby hunger.

Whether or not God grants you a child is not for me to say. Whether He blesses your womb and gives you a biological child or if He answers your desire with an adopted child, either way is a magnificent blessing unparalleled in man's abilities. But what can seem so impossible to those of us struggling with infertility, God **_can_** bless you with a happy, fulfilled, **_complete_** life even without children. I think this can be even harder to believe sometimes, but it is absolutely true.

My prayer for you is that you know deep down inside that God is able, He is willing and He will do for you what no other power can do. He understands your baby hunger. Your infertility does not intimidate Him. In fact, He knew your lot in life long before any physician ever diagnosed it. He knew it when He placed the burning desire for a child deep within you. He has never yet said, "Well, my goodness! Maybe I shouldn't have placed that emotion there!" He has never once been "shocked"! I love the way comedian Mark Lowry puts it—"Has it ever occurred to you that nothing ever occurs to God?" He can use your heartache to bring healing to you and to others. He can use your shortcomings to showcase His abilities and He can use your void to bring about fullness of joy!

If childlessness is the path you are walking, rest in the knowledge that this Scripture never once said, "I've come that they might have life and have it more abundantly when they have children". Remember, I think it's as important to see what is missing in Scripture as it is to see what is there. Aren't you glad that God didn't accidentally leave that phrase out? He can—and He will—grant you life more abundantly—even without children—if you will allow Him to do so. The only prerequisite to a more abundant life is life in Christ Himself. He has already done the work for you to provide this abundant life He has promised. There are so many promises from a God with a perfect track record. He will not—He cannot—fail you. It's simply not in His character.

In closing, I'd like to encourage you to continue to pray. Saturate this battle with prayer—every decision, every event, every day. Pray for yourselves—pray for the wisdom to know how to continue, whether to continue trying to conceive, to adopt, or to accept a childless life. Any of these can be in His perfect will for you. And pray for each other—strength to pursue the plan God has for you. Trust that He loves you and knows the perfect will for your life. He is an amazing God with an amazing plan. A God who understands your baby hunger and is standing with open arms to walk with you through this journey.

Things to remember about Rivers & Mountains:

- ➤ God is a God of the impossible! Nothing is too difficult for Him!
- ➤ Christ has provided for you life more abundantly.
- ➤ God's promises to you are true whether or not you have children.
- ➤ Saturate your infertility story with prayer.

APPENDIX A

Discussion Guide

The following is offered as a means to help you begin to explore your feelings about what you have read. This discussion guide can be used as part of your own personal devotions or as a catalyst for a dialogue with others who are living an experience similar to your own. 2 Corinthians 1:4 tells us that we will be able to comfort those who are in any affliction with the comfort with which we are comforted by God! In joining with others who are walking the same road, may you find peace and healing for yourself and others. You may want to jot your responses down either on these pages or in a journal and come back to them in the weeks and months ahead. This is a wonderful way to realize just how God is working and moving throughout your story!

If you are interested in starting a Christian Support for Infertility & Child Loss Group in your area, please feel free to contact *Sarah's Laughter* for help and guidelines. We will be happy to offer support, encouragement and suggestions for a successful support system.

Contact us at

Sarah's Laughter
Christian Infertility Support
36317 Maple Leaf Ave.
Prairieville, LA 70769
supportgroup@Sarahs-laughter.com

Abraham & Sarah

1. How do you relate to Abraham? To Sarah?

2. Abraham felt that nothing mattered as long as he had no heir to give his name to. Why is it so easy to feel this way? When have you felt this way?

3. How has God used what you understand the most to teach you what you understand the least?

4. Sarah laughed in disbelief at the promises of God. How has your disbelief manifested itself? What is the difference in doubt and disbelief? List several Scriptures to help you when it is difficult to believe.

5. How does knowing that God will work things out at the appointed time help you in your struggle? Discuss a time when you've seen God move and you've known the timing was within His plan.

6. How has infertility taken away your laughter? How would you like to see God give you your laughter back?

Jacob & Rachel

1. How do you relate to Jacob? To Rachel?

2. How has your marriage been affected by infertility? What has been the most frustrating aspect of this journey?

3. Relationships with family and friends are often touched by infertility. How have these precious relationships changed since you first realized that having children would be difficult? What helpful things have friends and family done? What hurtful things have they done? How can you better communicate with them?

4. 2 Corinthians 10:5 tells us we can take our thoughts and make them captive to Jesus Christ. Spend some time noticing your thoughts. Are there more negative thoughts than positive thoughts? How can you make those thoughts captive to Jesus? How do you plan on replacing those damaging thoughts with uplifting ones?

5. Read Isaiah 62:5. Describe how you would love to see God rejoice over you. Read Zephaniah 3:17. The NIV says that He will rejoice over you with singing. What song do you think He sings over you?

6. What conscious decisions will you make in order to choose joy?

Elkanah & Hannah

1. How do you relate to Elkanah? To Hannah?

2. How do you feel the world around you has been like Peninnah or Eli? Find at least three Scriptures to comfort you when you feel provoked or misunderstood.

3. Describe the significance of a double portion. How has God granted you a double portion throughout your struggle?

4. Purpose-full infertility. How could God have a holy purpose in your battle?

5. What must you do within yourself to be able to totally release the burden of your infertility to the Lord? Why would you want to?

6. Hannah's praise to God outnumbered her petitions to God. What is your ratio of petition to praise? How can you increase praise in your life? More quiet time? Decide when and where that will be. More attention to lack of praise in your prayer life? Make a written list of things for which to be thankful.

Zacharias & Elizabeth

1. How do you relate to Zacharias? To Elizabeth?

2. Why do you think Zacharias had such a hard time believing the wonderful news announced by Gabriel?

3. Many people believe infertility is a curse. What do you believe? How does the story of Zacharias and Elizabeth support or refute your view?

4. Why does God withhold children from righteous people yet give them to those who seem indifferent to them? How do you resolve this in your heart and mind?

5. Look at the lineage of Jesus. Why do you think God used children of barren wombs to create the earthly ancestry of Christ?

6. Should God choose to bless you with a child, whether from your body or from other means, what responsibility does this place on you? How would you ascertain that your child would be able to carry out God's perfect plan for his or her life?

Jason & Beth

1. How do you relate to Jason? To Beth?

2. How has God been the Prince of Peace to you throughout your infertility?

3. God turned my greatest sorrow into my greatest blessing. How has He—or *is* He—doing that for you?

4. What have you learned about your relationship with God since dealing with infertility? What have you learned about yourself?

5. What blessings have come to you through infertility?

<u>*Adoption*</u>

1. What are your views on adoption? Imagine the miraculous intervention it takes to place a child in the right family. How active do you believe God is in the process of adoption?

2. How do you view your adoption into God's family?

3. Just being God's child gives you unfathomable worth. You bring no value to the table. You just come bearing God's Name. Discuss how you feel when you think about your worth in God's eyes.

4. Imagine a home with an adopted and a biological child. Now imagine that that home is Heaven. What does it mean to you that you are a joint-heir with Jesus?

5. Describe a time that you know God has ordered your steps. How do you know? What does it feel like to know that the God of the universe ordered <u>*your*</u> steps?

Child Loss

1. How do you relate to David? To his servants?

2. How does the life of an unborn or newborn child so profoundly impact the life of a parent? Why does the loss of this life seem so devastating?

3. Where did David find the strength to worship so soon after the death of his child? How can you find that same strength?

4. God knows firsthand what it feels like to be the parent of a child who has died. How does this help you approach Him with your grief? How do you think God grieved the death of Jesus?

5. What have you done—or plan to do—to memorialize the life of the child you have lost?

6. Visualize your arrival in Heaven. Describe the very first moment you lay eyes on the child you lost on earth. What are you feeling? What are you saying? What do you see and hear? Who is around you? What does God say to you? What does your child look like? How do you begin to thank God for this marvelous reunion?

Rivers & Mountains

1. Does infertility seem more like a river or a mountain to you? Explain.

2. Read Genesis 18:14 and Luke 1:37. Do you truly believe that nothing is impossible with God? What has seemed impossible to you?

3. Are you living an abundant life right now? If you were instantly transformed into a person living an abundant life, what would be different?

4. Do you believe your life could be complete with fewer children than you originally planned? With an adopted child(ren)? Without children?

5. Make out a new prayer list. Include the issues you have been praying about as well as those you now realize you need to include. Commit to bringing each of these things to your Father in prayer, beginning today.

APPENDIX B

Encouraging Scriptures

There can be no greater source of encouragement throughout any battle than the powerful Word of God. It has never failed. It will never fail. Any promise written on those holy pages is infallible. You can bank your life and your eternity on those words.

The following Scriptures are given as suggestions for you to meditate on as you deal with infertility and the struggle that it brings. Psalm 119:105 tells us that the Word of God is a lamp unto our feet and a light unto our paths. Sometimes your path may grow dim and you cannot see where to turn. Turn to Scripture. Proverbs 30:5 tells us that every word of God is tested; He is a shield to those who take refuge in Him. When you're hurting, don't run from God. Run to Him as hard and fast as you can. He'll become a shield around you.

Memorize these words. Write them on your heart. Keep the Word of God in front of you all the time. I have scriptures written on business cards taped to my bathroom mirror. Every time I brush my teeth, there are God's promises staring me in the face! The scriptures tacked by the door to my garage remind me of God's provision and protection every time I enter or exit my home. The verses tucked away inside my wallet is a constant reminder each time I pull out a dollar bill or write a check. You will defeat Satan with the Word. Make it a integral part of your battle.

"Is anything too difficult for the LORD?..." Genesis 18:14

"For nothing will be impossible with God." Matthew 1:37

"I am come that they might have life, and that they might have it more abundantly." John 10:10 (KJV)

"For I know the plans I have for you," declares the LORD , "plans to prosper you and not to harm you, plans to give you hope and a future." Jeremiah 29:11 (NIV)

"Behold, I am the LORD, the God of all flesh; is anything too difficult for Me?" Jeremiah 32:27

"...lo, I am with you always..." Matthew 28:20

"Behold, children are a gift of the LORD, The fruit of the womb is a reward." Psalm 127:3

"For we do not have a high priest who cannot sympathize with our weaknesses, but One who has been tempted in all things as we are, yet without sin. Therefore let us draw near with confidence to the throne of grace, so that we may receive mercy and find grace to help in time of need." Hebrews 4:15, 16

"For as the rain and the snow come down from heaven and do not return there without watering the earth and making it bear and sprout, and furnishing seed to the sower and bread to the eater; So will My word be which goes forth from My mouth; It will not return to Me empty, without accomplishing what I desire and without succeeding in the matter for which I sent it." Isaiah 55:10-11

"Commit your way to the LORD, Trust also in Him, and He will do it." Psalm 37:5

"...we are taking every thought captive to the obedience of Christ," 2 Corinthians 10:5

"...And as the bridegroom rejoices over the bride, so your God will rejoice over you." Isaiah 62:5

"Hope deferred makes the heart sick, but desire fulfilled is a tree of life." Proverbs 13:12

"You have taken account of my wanderings; put my tears in Your bottle. Are they not in Your book?" Psalm 56:8

"Behold, I have inscribed you on the palms of My hands;" Isaiah 49:16

"Trust in the LORD with all your heart and do not lean on your own understanding. In all your ways acknowledge Him, and He will make your paths straight." Proverbs 3:5-6

"The steps of a man are established by the LORD, and He delights in his way." Psalm 37:23

"Now faith is the assurance of things hoped for, the conviction of things not seen." Hebrews 11:1

"Those who sow in tears shall reap with joyful shouting. Psalm 126:5

"So the ransomed of the LORD will return and come with joyful shouting to Zion, and everlasting joy will be on their heads. They will obtain gladness and joy, and sorrow and sighing will flee away." Isaiah 51:11

"This is my comfort in my affliction, that Your word has revived me." Psalm 119:50

"...Do not be grieved, for the joy of the LORD is your strength." Nehemiah 8:10

Other scriptures encouraging to me:

_____

_____

_____

_____

_____

_____

_____

_____

APPENDIX C

Sarah's Laughter

Christian Support for Infertility & Child Loss

*S*arah's Laughter is a ministry dedicated to healing the hurts of those struggling with infertility and child loss. Many feel that no one understands their hurt and sorrow. Many are misunderstood. Family and clergy often feel helpless to assist because of the intensely personal nature of the struggle. Our ministry is striving to reach these precious people struggling with baby hunger and child loss, and to remind them of a God who loves them passionately and possesses the balm necessary to heal their wounds.

Sarah's Laughter desires to minister in a variety of ways:

Infertility Facts:
- Infertility has tripled since 1965.
- Approximately one of six American couples of child bearing age will face difficulty getting pregnant.
- There is very little support within the Christian community.

Plan of Action:
- One day and half day conferences are available.

- Encouragement offered on website: www.Sarahs-Laughter.com
- Baby Hunger: Biblical Encouragement For Those Struggling With Infertility

Child Loss Facts:
- Many couples experience mind-numbing grief with the death of their child.
- If there is no body to bury, the deceased child is often viewed as an "it" rather than a baby.
- Doctors have told their patients that they have nothing to put in their hands to assist them in their grief.
- Too many grieving families are met with insensitivity and misunderstanding.

Plan of Action:
- Rainbow Boxes—This gift is appropriate to present to parents immediately following the death of their baby to assist them in funeral preparation.
- Rainbow Bags—This gift is appropriate following the loss of a baby at any stage, when time has elapsed following the death and the notification of the loss, or if the family decides against a burial.
- Half-day conferences are available.

Rainbow Boxes and *Rainbow Bags* are available through the website and can be sent overnight if necessary.

To order, write or e-mail: Sarah's Laughter
order@Sarahs-laughter.com
36317 Maple Leaf Ave.
Prairieville, LA 70769